COLLECTOR'S
◄ STYLE GUIDE ►

ART DECO

Malcolm Haslam
was a dealer in decorative arts for four
years, and is a regular contributor to
antiques magazines. He is the author of
*Pottery, English Art Pottery 1865-1915,
Marks and Monograms of the Modern
Movement 1875-1930, The Real World of
the Surrealists, William Staite Murray* and
The Martin Brothers, Potters, and
co-author of *In The Deco Style* and
The Amazing Bugattis.

COLLECTOR'S STYLE GUIDE

ART DECO

Malcolm Haslam

Ballantine Books • New York

Library of Congress Catalog Card Number: 87-91508

ISBN: 0-345-34742-0

Cover design by Richard Aquan
Manufactured in Italy
First American Edition: March 1988
10 9 8 7 6 5 4 3 2 1

ACKNOWLEDGEMENTS

I would like to thank the following for their help: all the dealers in Antiquarius who have lent
objects to be photographed; the Pruskin Gallery; John Jesse & Irina Laski; Sotheby's; Phillips;
Christie's; and Bonham's.
I am very grateful to Margaret Knight of the Victoria and Albert Museum who has contributed the
chapters on Fashion & Accessories, Metalwork & Jewellery, and Furniture & Textiles.

Malcolm Haslam

Picture credits for the Introduction
p.6 Sotheby's; p.8 Hulton Picture Library; p.9 Popperfoto; p.10 Architectural Association;
p.11 Sotheby's; p.12 Popperfoto; p.13 Hulton Picture Library; p.14 Architectural Association;
p.15 (top) Sotheby's, (bottom) Victoria & Albert Museum, London.

Author's note on the Price Lists
The price lists are based on auction prices recorded during the last two years in European and
American salerooms. For the purposes of the lists, £1 = $1.60.
The price band given is only a guide. If an item is found which is priced below the lower price given,
collectors should make sure that it is genuine, and not damaged or restored. If, on the other hand,
the price being asked is higher than the top price given in the list, collectors should ask themselves if
the object is of particularly fine quality, particularly large of its sort, very rare, or has some other
exceptional feature.
The figure indicating quality of design and/or decoration is largely subjective, and the collector will
no doubt find it entertaining to compare his/her own taste with the author's.

CONTENTS

INTRODUCTION

**Bronze and ivory figure by
Demetre Chiparus.**

Although born in the twenties, Art Deco belongs to our era. It was the style which first reflected today's attitudes to life, love and money. Since the First World War there has, of course, been the Second World War; man has landed on the Moon; penicillin and the microchip have been invented. But despite all the changes of the last seventy years, a time traveller from the present day would feel at home in the twenties, whereas the years before the First World War would seem totally alien to him. Modern consciousness was born on those battlefields; many of the artists and designers who contributed to Art Deco had learnt as much at the front as they had in any life class.

Many of the questions that preoccupied twenties culture still concern us today. Women's rights, extra-marital relationships and the misuse of narcotics are issues which agitate our minds now, just as they bothered people then. Eugene O'Neill's *Emperor Jones*, first performed in 1921, aired the problems that surround blacks in a white society, and Karel Čapek's *R.U.R.*, first performed in 1923, raised the issue of increasing unemployment in an era of machines. Neither of those two dragons has yet been slain. In a lighter vein, people in the 1920s talked as excitedly as we might today about the new Hollywood spectacular, the latest records and the next Wimbledon champions.

An aspect of life today which is particularly relevant to Art Deco is commercial competition. Then, as now, manufacturers and their advertising agents wooed customers, trying to win a greater share of the market. Then, as now, goods which were designed better than those offered by the competition usually sold

better. Then, as now, governments encouraged manufacturers to export so that the national balance of payments was improved. To this end, subsidies were provided to help finance trade promotions. One such subsidy, given by the Ministry of Commerce and Industry in France, sponsored the Exposition des Arts Décoratifs et Industriels Modernes, held in Paris from April to October 1925. The French abbreviated the Exhibition's unwieldy title to 'les Arts Décos': unwittingly – as usually happens – they had named a style.

THE 1925 EXHIBITION

Even though there was more than one style on display at the 1925 Exhibition, it must have been apparent to most visitors that one style in particular prevailed among the French exhibits. Everywhere, the oval and the octagon were to be seen; everywhere, there were graceful, slightly stylized, female nudes; and everywhere, in bronze, iron, glass, ceramic and marquetry, there were tightly packed flower-heads in baskets, bouquets and garlands. Other pervasive motifs were fronds, spirals, lightning flashes and ziggurats. On vases, screens and damasks, deer grazed or gambolled among slender tree trunks and doves perched on boughs.

This distinctive style was officially encouraged at the Exhibition by the sponsoring Ministry. It therefore dominated not only the pavilions of the state-owned Sèvres porcelain factory but also those of designers such as Ruhlmann, Brandt, Lalique, the Compagnie des Arts Français, and many others. The same style was propagated in the wares of the leading Parisian department stores. Four

Paris Exhibition 1925: the pavilion of La Maîtrise, the decorating studio of the department store Galeries Lafayette.

of them had opened design studios: Primavera, in the Printemps store; La Maîtrise, in Galeries Lafayette; Pomone, in Bon Marché; and Studium-Louvre, in Les Grands Magasins du Louvre. At these studios householders could buy furniture, curtains, carpets, crockery and ornaments in the same style, turning each room of their homes into an *ensemble*. The four studios had prominent pavilions at the Exhibition.

The Exhibition also contained a contribution from the Société des Artistes Décorateurs, a semi-official organization of designers – a series of rooms for an imaginary French embassy. Most of these rooms were decorated in the prevailing style, but in one or two a different aspect of Art Deco was evident. The smoking-room, for example, was designed by the architect Francis Jourdain, whose outlook was more advanced than the official taste. The décor

featured a red lacquer screen made by Jean Dunand and decorated with an almost abstract, geometrical design by Jean Lambert-Rucki. A Cubist sculpture by Jan and Jöel Martel stood on a cupboard. The whole *ensemble* must have tried the forbearance of Paul Léon, director of the Beaux-Arts and assistant commissioner-general of the Exhibition, and two large decorative panels in the embassy's entrance-hall, painted by the Cubist artists Robert Delaunay and Fernand Léger, proved too much for him: he ordered them to be removed.

CUBISM AND THE NEGRO/ AFRICAN INFLUENCE

Cubism, invented by Picasso and Braque before the First World War, had been assimilated by many artists and designers by the mid-1920s. 'Cubism is a decorative art,' wrote the picture dealer René Gimpel in 1930, 'though the Cubists didn't suspect this at the outset.' Some Art Deco designers borrowed elements from Cubism, such as distortion, angularity, geometrical arrangements, and features of African sculpture. The couturier Jacques Doucet collected Cubist paintings and, at the same time, examples of the African tribal art that had had such a powerful effect on Picasso and Braque. He commissioned Art Deco designers to create pieces of furniture which reflected the style of his African artefacts.

African, or rather Negro, culture also penetrated the arts of the twenties by another route – jazz. Jazz came to France with the American army in 1917. The next year, men of the 369th Regiment (otherwise known as 'the Harlem Hellfighters') provided a jazz band at one of Count Etienne de Beaumont's *fêtes* given in the garden of his Paris home. After the First World War the Jazz Age moved into full swing. Every fashionable Paris bar had its black pianist. In 1923 a jazz ballet called *La Création du Monde*, written by Darius Milhaud and with sets and costumes designed by Léger, was performed at the Théâtre des Champs-Elysées. On the same stage two years later Josephine Baker danced and clowned in the *Revue Nègre*. Jazz influenced the decorative arts, too, translated into striking colour harmonies and 'syncopated' linear rhythms.

LUXURIOUS DECO

French Art Deco was undoubtedly directed at the rich. The 1925 Paris Exhibition was intended to establish France as the principal, if not the only, purveyor of luxury goods to the wealthy. The materials used in these goods were exotic: gold leaf, lacquer, shagreen, mother of pearl, ivory, ebony, macassar, palmwood etc. The craftsmanship was painstaking and exquisite. For instance, to lacquer a surface, Dunand would apply twenty coats; between each application there had to be a polishing and four days of seasoning. 'So you'll understand,' he said to Gimpel, 'it's a positively Oriental labour.'

Art Deco in France was also closely connected with the Paris fashion houses. In 1912, for example, the couturier Paul Poiret established the Atelier Martine, which produced designs for furniture, metalwork and ceramics as well as fabrics. The

Josephine Baker.

9

Parisian dress designers have always pampered their clients, and Poiret more than most. Interiors created by the Martine studio were unashamedly luxurious. The actor Sacha Guitry ordered from Martine a sunken bathtub which was lined with gilt mosaic. 'Enough of privation!' he exclaimed. Other couturiers, such as Jeanne Lanvin, Suzanne Talbot and Jacques Doucet, also became leading patrons of the Art Deco designers and the style became as chic as high fashion.

Perhaps not surprisingly, it also reflected feminine taste. The influence of women was growing at that time, partly because of the continuing pressure for women's rights and partly because, after the slaughter of men in the First World War, there was a much larger than usual preponderance of women in Western Europe. In 1924 the Union des Arts Décoratifs, a body run by the government, organized an exhibition on the theme of a lady's boudoir, in which all the leading *ensembliers* participated. At the 1925 Exhibition, apart from the *chambres de femme* of the four department-store design studios, and the French embassy, there were pavilions devoted exclusively to women's fashion, jewellery and scent.

LE CORBUSIER AND THE ESPRIT NOUVEAU

In an obscure corner of the Exhibition, tucked away between two wings of the mighty Grand Palais, there was a modern villa designed by Le Corbusier, called the Pavillon d'Esprit Nouveau. The name referred to a magazine edited by the architect in which he had expressed his uncompromising antipathy to ornament. 'Modern decorative art', he had declared, 'has no décor.' The pavilion's interior was spartan compared with the ornate confections prepared by Ruhlmann and the other *ensembliers*. The walls were bare, apart from a model aeroplane and a few Cubist paintings. One or two thin rugs were laid on the floors. Simple bentwood chairs manufactured by Thonet and office furniture made by Roneo were all that the rooms contained, except for a sculpture or two by Jacques Lipchitz. No greater contrast to the luxurious interiors elsewhere in the Exhibition could be imagined; yet Le Corbusier's pavilion contributed its own share to the sum of Art Deco.

The organizers of the Exhibition did not like Le Corbusier's pavilion

Villa Savoye, Poissy, designed by Le Corbusier, 1929 – 1931.

A view of the stairway inside the Villa Savoye.

any more than they liked Léger's and Delaunay's panels. On 10 July, the day it was officially opened by M. de Monzie, the Minister of Beaux-Arts, they had a fence six metres high erected round it. Cubism and the modern styles of architecture related to it were alien to the French artistic establishment. Picasso was Spanish; Daniel Kahnweiler, the dealer who had promoted Cubist painting in its infancy, was German; and Le Corbusier himself was Swiss. No doubt the Beaux-Arts officials had heard that the architecture of the Pavillon d'Esprit Nouveau was related to developments beyond the Rhine. Hatred of *les sales Boches* still ran high in nationalist circles, and Germany had not been invited to participate at all in the Paris Exhibition.

The leading European architects of the time – from Germany, Austria, Holland and France – were united, however, as was evident in their reaction to the results of the competition held by the League of Nations for the design of a headquarters building in Geneva. In May 1927 it was announced that Le Corbusier had been awarded the first prize. But the French delegate protested immediately: Le Corbusier was disqualified on a technicality, and in December the job was awarded to the French academic architect Paul Nénot. It became apparent to the Modernists that an international organization should be set up to propagate their views and defend their interests. A meeting was arranged for June 1928 at the château of La Sarraz in Vaud, Switzerland.

Among those who attended the meeting at La Sarraz were some of the most notable figures in the history of twentieth-century design. They included the Dutch architect

'Flame dancer', a bronze and ivory figure by Ferdinand Preiss.

H.P. Berlage, who was then over seventy and had been involved in the movement to reform architecture and design at the turn of the century, and Gerrit van Rietveld, another Dutchman, who had designed the Red-Blue chair in 1917 and was a member of the De Stijl group of artists. As well as Le Corbusier, there was Pierre Chareau from Paris, who had contributed a study-library to the French

11

Paul Poiret.

embassy interiors at the 1925 Exhibition, and had worked for Jacques Doucet. From Frankfurt came Ernst May. The housing estates which May and his colleagues had designed were revolutionary both in the style of architecture and in its universal application. May's office had designed everything, including – literally – the kitchen sinks. May had even compiled the 'Frankfurt Register', which listed items of modern furniture and lighting fixtures recommended to tenants. The result was an *ensemble* – a very different one to those furnished by Primavera or La Maîtrise, and based on a very different rationale, but still an *ensemble*.

The eventual consequence of the coming together of so many eminent Modernists was the establishment of the Union des Artistes Modernes. This was founded in 1930 by, among others, Pierre Chareau, Francis Jourdain and Le Corbusier.

BAUHAUS MODERNISM AND AMERICA

Le Corbusier's Esprit Nouveau and Modernist antipathy to decoration were profoundly influenced by the Bauhaus. The aim of its founder, Walter Gropius, was to supply industry with designs and designers as well as turning out architects who would disseminate the modern style. Tubular steel furniture designed by Marcel Breuer, head of the cabinet-making department, was manufactured in limited quantities, but much more successful Bauhaus designs for mass-production were the glass and metal lamps designed by Marianne Brandt for Körting & Matthiessen and by Adolf Meyer for Zeiss Ikon. Gradually the Bauhaus style spread into glassware, ceramics, posters, books and typography.

Oskar Schlemmer, who directed the theatre workshop at the Bauhaus, noted in his diary shortly after the school had moved to Dessau in 1925: 'The artistic climate here cannot support anything that is not the latest, the most modern, up-to-the-minute.... Jazz, hectic pace, movies, America, airplanes, the automobile. Those are the terms in which people here think.' Four years later an American advertising executive wrote that he considered the successful businessmen to be the ones who had 'caught the new tempo, jumped in at the right time to capitalize on the swing to colour, the acceptance of radio, the short skirt, the craze for speed ... the public's discovery that it could have its 1940 luxuries today on the instalment plan.'

Many American manufacturers found it hard to keep up with the changing fashions. When Howard

Carter discovered Tutankhamun's tomb in 1922, there was a clamour for Egyptian-style jewellery and clothing. (A syndicate of Parisian couturiers even offered Carter £20,000 for the right to copy the clothing and ornament discovered in the tomb.) Cheney Brothers, a firm of textile manufacturers, sent a fashion designer to Egypt to make sketches. But before the designer had returned, the craze was over. Cheney's also tried to anticipate fashion, introducing the 'Ferronière' line of prints based on motifs from Edgar Brandt's ironwork in 1924, a year before the Paris Exhibition.

It was probably a feeling of remoteness from European trends which dissuaded the American authorities from accepting an invitation to participate in the Exhibition. But before 1925 had ended, the influence of the Paris show was evident in New York stores. Saks Fifth Avenue introduced a 'new modernistic décor' for its window displays and interiors. Soon Cheney's employed Brandt himself to work on the decoration of its stores. In 1927 Macy's held its Art-in-Trade Exposition, which featured modern furnishings from Europe and the USA.

Many American designers were impressed by Le Corbusier's modern vision, and by the work of artists such as Paul Frankl and Donald Deskey, whose style was infused with

Jazz band performing in the 1920s; the young **Duke Ellington** is in the centre of the front row.

Bauhaus workshop block at Dessau, designed by Walter Gropius.

a warmth not found in the austerity of the Bauhaus. Many of Deskey's motifs refer directly to Léger's Cubist paintings, and Frankl's furniture and Deskey's work at the Radio City Music Hall in New York City corresponds visually to designs by members of the Union des Artistes Modernes.

The tentative efforts of Bauhaus designers to work for industry were overshadowed by the rise of the product designer in the USA during the late 1920s and the 1930s. Walter Dorwin Teague, Raymond Loewy, Norman Bel Geddes and Henry Dreyfuss designed not only traditional items such as glassware, ceramics, metalwork and furniture, but also the products of new technology: automobiles, telephones, cameras, duplicators, refrigerators, toasters, radios etc. The streamlined style which they created had in common with other types of Art Deco the underlying idea of the *ensemble*. By surrounding themselves with streamlined goods and appliances, American consumers felt they were up-to-date, living in a modern world free from poverty and privation. This optimism survived the Depression, and the streamlined style received its greatest accolade in 1939 when it dominated the New York World's Fair, just as fourteen years earlier the original Art Deco had prevailed at the Exhibition in Paris.

Enamelled copper vase by Camille Fauré decorated in an abstract style widespread in Europe during the later twenties.

Watercolour design for a rug by Edward McKnight Kauffer, an American artist who worked in England and was influenced by Cubist painting.

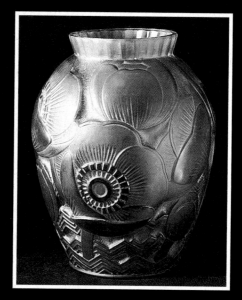

CHAPTER ONE

GLASS

Vase by Paul d'Avesn. Steve Johnson,
T4 Antiquarius, London. Price: £220.

Lalique scent bottles
Height (tallest): 13.75cm
Sold: Sotheby's, London, 16/5/86
Price: £550

'Fit Triplex and be safe,' read a cable from England addressed to Henry Ford immediately after he had been involved in a car crash in 1927. The demand for toughened, unsplinterable glass came not only from the automobile and aeroplane industries, however, but also from architects and even furniture makers. Whether buildings were designed round a steel skeleton or whether they were still constructed on the old system of load-bearing walls, glass during the twenties and thirties was a more generally used building material than ever before. There were glass floor-blocks, glass bricks, glass ceilings; windows grew until they were whole walls. Between 1928 and 1931 the French architect Pierre Chareau built an entire 'maison de verre' for Jean Dalsace on the rue Saint-Guillaume in Paris. Glass architecture was symptomatic of an era which welcomed the sun's rays, previously regarded as injurious to health. It suited a generation which liked to be out of doors.

The strengthened plate-glass that became available during the twenties was used in the manufacture of furniture too. When tubular steel was

Lalique vase
Height: 19.2cm
Galia Antiques, Q4/5 Antiquarius,
London
Price: £800

evokes the mood of the period. A famous print by Louis Icart, a dry-point and etching of 1932 called *Le Cocktail*, shows a flapper sheathed in a backless chiffon gown, her hair shingled, her forearm encircled by bangles and a fur-collared evening coat hitched over one shoulder, lolling not so elegantly on a bar stool. Her right hand clutches an empty cocktail glass loosely. Its plain stem terminates in a small sphere from which rises a broad, inverted glass cone. This is the classic Art Deco cocktail glass, the geometry of its forms ready to be complemented by the larger sphere of an olive or a cherry bisected by the straight line of a cocktail stick. Such glasses are not rare, having been manufactured in enormous quantities to this day, but

permitted in the domestic interior, towards the end of the 1920s, glass was used for shelving and table-tops; tubular steel tables made by Thonet had glass tops manufactured by the Venetian firm of Barovier; Pierre Legrain designed a grand piano, the case and legs of which were made of plate glass; the novelist Beverley Nichols reported 'staircases with glass banisters' featured in the modish interior. Mirror glass, too, was widely used on furniture, and the ubiquitous cocktail cabinet was often lined with it.

COCKTAIL GLASSES AND SCENT BOTTLES

Just as the cocktail cabinet and the dressing table are *par excellence* the items of furniture which typify the Art Deco style, so the cocktail glass more than any other item of glassware, except perhaps the scent bottle,

Perfume bottle designed by Süe et Mare
Height: 21.5cm
Sold: Sotheby's, London, 16/5/86
Price: (set of three) £550

19

probably few date from the inter-war years. So many of them, like their users, must have taken that one Sidecar too many, and finished in splinters on the bar-room floor.

Art Deco scent bottles are to be found in profusion. Chunkier than cocktail glasses, and less prone to accident anyway, they have survived in all shapes and sizes. Towards the end of the nineteenth century, advances in organic chemistry made possible the production of synthetic perfumes. A far wider range of scents became available and the different varieties vied with each other in the market-place.

François Coty seems to have been the first *parfumier* to realize that a scent could be given a competitive edge by its packaging. In 1907 he commissioned the jeweller René Lalique, who was turning more and more to the medium of glass, to design bottles for his perfume. They were the first of a number of scent bottles Lalique designed over the next thirty years, many of them for specific brands produced by cosmetic houses and parfumiers such as Roger & Gallet, d'Orsay, Arys and Houbigant, while others were created for general use on the dressing table.

Usually moulded with flowers, female figures, animals or insects, Lalique's bottles spawned a host of imitations which vary widely in quality of design and execution. The French firm of Baccarat, for instance, produced a bottle for d'Orsay's perfume *Toujours Fidèle*, with the stopper moulded as a dog, probably designed by Georges Chevalier. Like many Lalique bottles this Baccarat example was given a decorative staining. Most of the Lalique imitations do not aspire to such sophistication, but many were made in

Lalique 'Bellecour' vase
Height: 28.5cm
Sold: Phillips, London, 13/3/86
Price: £968

coloured glass and some have moulded stoppers in the form of women more or less draped with lengths of material, pierrots and such *dramatis personae* of the Art Deco spectacular.

Apart from the creations of Lalique and his followers, which are a distinct type of Art Deco glass, there are three other categories of glass, each clearly exemplified by scent bottles: enamelled glass, glass designed by artists outside the industry, and glass created by individual studios.

When the couturier Paul Poiret entered the perfume business in 1911 he designed his own packaging, including one bottle made for his scent *Fanfan la Tulipe*, which was decorated with tulips painted in enamel. During the Art Deco period a lot of glass, particularly in France, was given this sort of decoration. Louis Vuitton, purveyor of luxury goods such as fitted cabin trunks, produced scent bottles, usually with tops of silver, carved wood or ivory, painted in enamel with, for example, representations of dancers from the Ballets Russes. Another, very popular, type of enamelled scent-bottle was the sort given a geometrical shape, either moulded or cut, and decorated in black enamel with an abstract, geometrical design. Baccarat made these, and huge quantities of them were produced in the glasshouses of Czechoslovakia. Many such bottles were atomizers; some still have their original bulbs and tassels, adding much to their period charm and a little, perhaps, to their market value.

Another category of Art Deco glass comprises those pieces where the principal artistic input is the design of the shape, furnished by a designer from outside the glass industry. For example, Süe et Mare, the architect and painter partnership specializing in the design of de luxe furniture and fittings, produced a set of black cut glass scent bottles in three sizes; and the English firm of glass manufacturers Steven & Williams commissioned the New Zealand-born architect Keith Murray to design a

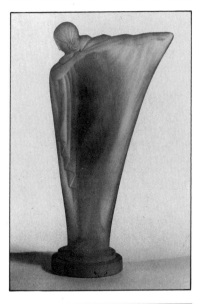

Etling opalescent glass figure
Height: 20.5cm
Sold: Phillips, London, 19/6/86
Price: £462

Table lamp with Robj shade
Height: 25cm
Sold: Phillips, London, 19/6/86
Price: £396

Enamelled liqueur set
Height (decanter): 20.9cm
Galia Antiques, Q4/5 Antiquarius,
London
Price (decanter + 6 glasses): £360

wide range of glassware, including scent bottles.

The final category of Art Deco glass, known as studio glass, is the work of individual glass artists. This is something of a cheat in this section because, although many of the pieces made by Maurice Marinot, the greatest of the glass artists, were in the form of a *flacon* (the word used by the French for a scent bottle), they were certainly never intended to actually hold perfume.

LALIQUE AND HIS IMITATORS

Lalique held his first exhibition of glass in 1912. Most of these early

Hanging lamp with Muller Frères shade
Height: 73cm
Sold: Bonham's, London, 5/12/86
Price: £286

pieces, however, gave little hint of what was to be produced after the First World War at the factory in Wingen-sur-Moder, which Lalique bought in 1918. Here, using *demi-cristal* (which had never been considered glass of good quality) and industrial processes such as blowing into moulds and the stamping press, Lalique produced a wide range of articles – including vases, bowls, lampshades, trays, clock-cases, ashtrays, scent bottles, and items of tableware such as decanters, jugs and glasses.

Lalique's style is very individual, sometimes echoing the mannerisms of Art Nouveau, but more often adopting the forms or motifs of Art Deco. The most highly prized pieces are those which most strongly represent his own version of Art Deco, and some models are seldom found at affordable prices, especially when they are made of coloured glass. Another important criterion of value is the rarity of any particular model. Many pieces designed during the 1920s and 1930s are still in production today, which has the effect of fixing their value at or near the current retail price. Glass produced since 1945 is marked 'Lalique France', pre-War glass is usually marked 'R. Lalique' in capitals, and early examples were signed 'R. Lalique France' in script with a model number.

Such was Lalique's commercial success that many firms imitated his products. In France there was Hunebelle, whose moulded decoration tended to be more geometrical than Lalique's. The glassworks of

Baccarat candlesticks
Height: 7.5cm
Galia Antiques, Q4/5 Antiquarius, London
Price: £175

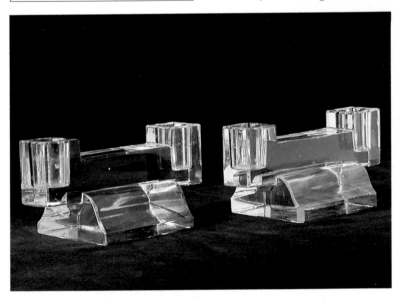

**Enamelled decanters and
liqueur glasses**
Height (taller decanter): 21 cm
Sold: Christie's South Kensington,
London, 19/9/86
Price (16 items): £660

Marius-Ernest Sabino, although imitating Lalique's technique, tried to be artistically independent, and the same may be said for the glass of Paul d'Avesn. The Parisian firm of Etling, which commissioned and retailed bronze and ivory statuettes, also dealt in glassware, most of it designed by Geneviève Granger and Lucille Sevin along the lines of Lalique's nude female figures. Robj, whose entrepreneurial role was similar to Etling's, sold glass in the style of Lalique, particularly lampshades. French manufacturers of similar lampshades were Muller Frères, Verlys and Schneider. In Belgium during the 1930s the Val St Lambert glassworks produced wares in the style of Lalique, called 'Luxval' and designed by Charles Graffart and René Delvenne. The Consolidated Lamp and Glass Company of Coraopolis, Pennsylvania, USA, manufactured vases and lamp bases which were close, sometimes exact, copies of Lalique originals, and the Phoenix Glass Company of Monaca, a few miles north of Coraopolis, produced poor quality imitations of glassware by Hunebelle, Etling and Verlys.

British imitations of Lalique included the car mascots made by the firm of Red-Ashay. Lalique's car mascots are fiercely fought over in the saleroom; they fetch thousands rather than hundreds of pounds, except for the very dull St Christopher mascot. The Red-Ashay models are often lightly clad female figures, their hair streaming in the wind, similar to one of Lalique's mascots but usually less than a quarter the price. There is also a Red-Ashay mascot in the form of a Pharaoh's head, not directly related to any Lalique model. Other British glass in the style of Lalique was made by the Sunderland firm of James Jobling (vases, bowls etc.), and John Walsh of Birmingham (lampshades).

ENAMELLED GLASS

Enamelling was a particularly popular mode of decorating numerous glass objects during the 1920s. The style of the Ecole de Paris, a sort of amalgam of Fauvism and Cubism, was an important tributary to the mainstream of Art Deco, and the designs enamelled on French glassware often show characteristics of contemporary painting and graphic art. Marcel Goupy, the artistic director of Georges Rouard's gallery in the avenue de l'Opéra from 1909 to 1954, designed both the shapes and decoration of enamelled glass vases, bowls and boxes. Some of these show strongly neo-classical mythological scenes in tune with much of French art during the post-war years. Others feature stylized flowers, ladies à la mode or landscapes incorporating such Art Deco characteristics as cypress trees, billowing clouds and weeping willows.

Between 1919 and 1923, Goupy's designs were executed by Auguste Heiligenstein who had learnt his skills at the Legras and Baccarat factories, but pieces always bear Goupy's name. Subsequently Heiligenstein independently made and decorated enamelled glassware which he signed with his own name.

Like Rouard, Delvaux sold decorated glass and pottery, and had his own workshops. Enamelled glassware was decorated with designs incorporating flowers, birds or abstract patterns.

Jean Luce also designed enamelled decoration for the glassware which was sold in his father's Paris shop. The motifs were usually floral or geometrical.

Baccarat's sets of decanters and glasses were produced with the same style of decoration as its scent bottles. The more sophisticated enamel decoration found on some Baccarat glass of the Art Deco period was designed by Georges Chevalier or André Ballet.

Much of the glass produced by the Wiener Werkstätte was decorated with enamels. Artists who were apparently involved in the actual painting included Dagobert Peche, Mathilde Flogl, Hilda Jesser, Julius Zimpel and Reni Schaschl. Several

Wiener Werkstätte bowl and cover, enamelled by Reni Schaschl
Height: 12.75cm
Sold: Sotheby's, London, 16/5/86
Price: £440

Daum acid-cut vase
Height: 24.9cm
Moty & Anita, V14/15 Antiquarius,
London
Price: £325

Wiener Werkstätte artists also designed for the Viennese firm of J. & L. Lobmeyr which manufactured glass decorated with enamels by Lotte Fink. The style used by these Austrian artists incorporated more or less abstract floral motifs, often combined with a spikiness apparently related to Expressionist art, and sometimes arranged on a sort of irregular, rectilinear grid. The same style of decoration is seen on quantities of enamelled glassware produced at the Haida, Steinschönau and Jablonec technical schools in Czechoslovakia, and the Zwiesel technical school in Bavaria, Germany. At these schools, enamelling was often combined with engraving on the glassware.

DESIGNER'S GLASS

Foremost in the category of glassware where the primary artistic input was the design of the shape is the glass produced by the Bauhaus. Very little of this is available to the collector, however, and when it does appear on the market it inevitably fetches very high prices because of its art-historical significance.

Apart from scent bottles, the architect Keith Murray designed a wide range of vases, bowls and tableware for the Stourbridge firm of Stevens & Williams. Murray's shapes were simple and geometrical, sometimes decorated with cut designs. James Powell, the London glassmaker, followed Steven & Williams's lead, commissioning designs for tableware from the furniture maker Gordon Russell, who also designed for Stevens & Williams. This, too, has lightly cut decoration of, for instance, leaves and cow parsley.

In the USA, the industrial designer Walter Dorwin Teague was retained by the Steuben Glass company during the early 1930s to design several ranges of stemmed cylindrical drinking glasses. For Steuben he also designed a columnar candlestick, decorated with an etched spiral design. Teague later worked for the Libbey Glass Company, which commissioned designs from several outside artists.

Lobmeyr commissioned designs for tableware from the architects Josef Hoffmann, Otto Prutscher, Oswald Härdtl, Eduard Wimmer, and the potter Michael Powolny (who also designed for the firm Ludwig Moser). Other distinguished architects who designed shapes for glassware included Alvar Aalto, who worked for Karhule-Iittale in Finland, and the Dutch architect H.P. Berlage and Frank Lloyd Wright, who both worked for the Royal Dutch Glass-works at Leerdam. The resurgence of Venice as a centre of the glass industry during the 1930s was to a considerable extent due to architect Tommaso Buzzi's and sculptor Napoleone Martinuzzi's designs for Venini, and artist Vittorio Zecchin's designs for Cappellin-Venini and Fratelli Toso.

STUDIO GLASSWARE

During the 1920s there emerged the artist-craftsmen who worked in either pottery or glass. They worked independently, with perhaps one or two assistants, and what they made was not commercial, but rather an expression of themselves. As the leading French glass artist, Maurice Marinot, wrote: 'Painting and glass-work have their source in the joyful desire to create, through shape and colour, works whose birth is in feeling and whose completion is in reasoned order.' Marinot was a painter before he became a glass artist; he had been closely associated with the Fauves. His earliest glass was decorated with enamels, the designs of which were reminiscent of Matisse's paintings. As he mastered the medium, so his glass became increasingly sophisticated, both in technique and in artistic effect. Many of his vases and bottles are internally decorated with air bubbles and pieces of metal foil trapped in the glass. He wrought some of his decoration at the furnace, producing layers of crackled glass and sealing the effects of chemical reactions

Daum acid-cut vase
Height: 18.8cm
Steve Johnson, T4 Antiquarius,
London
Price: £190

within the glass. 'I think', wrote Marinot, 'that a beautiful piece of glass should keep as much as possible the aspect of the breath which creates it, and that its form should be a moment in the life of the glass fixed by the cooling.' Later he used deep acid etching to make geometrical patterns in high relief, such as chevrons and circles.

Alas, Marinot's glass is practically unobtainable. Much of it has gone to museums, either purchased during his lifetime or presented by his widow after his death. Some was destroyed when his studio was bombed in 1944. When a piece does

27

come on the market, Croesus might well be the underbidder. However, more available are examples of the glass made by Henri Navarre and André Thuret, both of whom were strongly influenced by Marinot.

Navarre was an experienced sculptor who went to the Conservatoire des Arts et Métiers in Paris to study stained glass and mosaic. There he met André Thuret, director of the Conservatoire and an engineer retained by a glassworks at Bezons. They were deeply impressed by Marinot's glass and began to experiment themselves at workshops in Bagneux near Fontainebleau. Both artists' work is reminiscent of Marinot's internally decorated glass, and they both used metallic oxides to produce an unprecedented range of colours in their glass. Pieces by Thuret and Navarre tend to be more expensive the closer they approach the technical and artistic qualities of Marinot's glass. Georges Dumoulin was another imitator of Marinot, but his work is less sophisticated than Thuret's or Navarre's. He frequently used applied and trailed glass to decorate his pieces.

ETCHED AND ENGRAVED GLASS

In France, towards the end of the 1920s there was a swing away from enamelling towards engraving, and at the same time decorative designs changed from floral and figurative to abstract geometrical. These tendencies occur in the work produced by the Daum factory, Marcel Goupy, Jean Luce and Louis Vuitton.

Aristide Colotte opened his own workshop at Nancy in 1927. He specialized in carving statues, often biblical figures, from solid crystal, and also produced deeply carved and

Daum vase, blown into iron mount
Height: 30cm
Sold: Sotheby's, London, 19/12/86
Price: £528

etched vases, some decorated with geometrical patterns, some with animals or figures. In Germany, Wilhelm von Eiff, who in 1922 was appointed professor in charge of cutting and engraving on glass and gemstones at Stuttgart Art School, made a range of vessels in simple, geometrical shapes, engraved with abstract designs, portraits and classical scenes. Similar techniques were used by Guido Balsamo-Stella, in Italy, but with very different results. Working in Venice, he had vessels made to his designs by the firm of Fratelli Toso. He decorated them with wheel-carved designs of animals, nude figures, mythological and genre scenes, sometimes treated humorously.

Balsamo-Stella's wife, Anna, was Swedish and she introduced him to the work of the Orrefors glassworks in Sweden. This firm's engraved glass gained an enormous reputation during the 1920s and 1930s. The principal artists working for it during this period were Edward Hald (a painter who had studied under Henri Matisse and whose style is close to that of the Ecole de Paris), Simon Gate (who worked in a more formal, ponderous manner) and Vicke Lindstrand (who did not join Orrefors until the 1930s and whose designs, often of bathers or athletes, reflected that decade's more substantial figurative style).

A glassworks that followed Orrefors's lead and produced glass decorated by wheel-engraving was the Steuben Glass Company, in the USA, which commissioned the sculptor Sidney Biehler Waugh to supply designs, but these pieces tend to be prohibitively expensive.

Stuart & Sons of Stourbridge, England, commissioned designs for engraved glass from the painters Paul Nash, Graham Sutherland, Laura Knight and Eric Ravilious. In Austria, Lobmeyr made glass engraved by Eva Rottenberg, who collaborated with Marianne Rath on some irregularly cut crystal vases also made by Lobmeyr. Engraved glass was also produced by the Czechoslovakian technical schools and by the Haida firm of Johann Oertel & Co.

CAMEO GLASS

Cameo glass, which had been the principal product of French glass-makers such as Gallé and Daum during the Art Nouveau period, continued to be made in the 1920s. Emile Gallé had died in 1904, but his glassworks in Nancy remained in production, making rather feeble attempts to manufacture cameo glass in the Art Deco style. Daum, however, made some very accomplished Art Deco cameo glass, which is usually very expensive. In 1921 André Delatte set up his workshops in Nancy. There he made cameo glass which reflected the past glories of that city too much to be considered truly Art Deco. Charles Schneider, who had worked as a designer for Daum and who had established a glassworks at Epinay-sur-Seine in 1913, made cameo glass during the

Pâte de verre **pendant**
Length: 6.7cm
Sold: Sotheby's, New York, 19/6/86
Price: $605

1920s which is decorated with stylized floral motifs or geometrical patterns in colours such as orange, turquoise, peppermint green and yellow. This was marketed under the name 'Charder' (an elliptical form of CHARles SchneiDER) or 'Le Verre Français'; some pieces are marked with both names.

The Legras factory in Saint-Denis produced cameo glass featuring less stylized decoration, often incorporating friezes of birds. Legras also made glass with the design painted on a surface mottled by acid, giving the appearance of cameo glass.

Muller Frères of Lunéville also made cameo glass often decorated with friezes of stylized animals, but they were incorporated in geometrical patterns, and the outer layer of glass often contained pieces of metal foil.

OTHER FORMS OF DECORATED GLASS

Schneider, Legras, Muller and Daum all made glass internally decorated with coloured glass, pieces of metal foil, or bubbles, or a combination of these. The production of this sort of glass was a direct result of Maurice Marinot's success, and although industrially manufactured pieces inevitably lack the individual expression of the artist's work, many of them are stylistically and aesthetically convincing. Auguste Heiligenstein was put in charge of the Legras factory's production of internally decorated glass which is marked 'Montjoye'. In Scotland the North British Glassworks employed the Catalan glassworker Salvador Ysart, from 1922, to supervise production of internally decorated coloured glass called 'Monart' ware. Daum, following Marinot's lead further, started to make glass vessels deeply acid etched with geometrical patterns. These were often made in coloured, typically amber, glass.

During the Art Deco period *pâte de verre* and *pâte de cristal*, which had been invented towards the end of the nineteenth century, reached peaks of technical and artistic perfection in the hands of François Décorchemont, Almaric Walter and Gabriel Argy-Rousseau. The nature of the process, which is a combination of pottery and glassmaking techniques, means that every piece of *pâte de verre* and *pâte de cristal* is unique, with the result that examples are never cheap. Décorchemont, who sold his work through Georges Rouard's gallery, made the most stylish and technically excellent pieces; they are seldom if ever available to the collector of modest means. Walter's and Argy-Rousseau's work is not much cheaper, but both made pendants and small *coupes* which are a little more affordable.

Drawn glass figures first gained their enormous popularity during the 1920s. Unfortunately, because of their fragility, few have survived from those years, but they occasionally appear and are usually not expensive. The Czechoslovakian artist Jaroslav Brychta made charming drawn glass figures of nymphs, fauns and inebriated gentlemen in evening dress. For the Bimini Werkstätte in Vienna, A. and J. Berger and Fritz Lampl made blown glass figurines, including highly stylized sportsmen such as skiers and fencers.

Nymphs, revellers, sportsmen – all were very much Art Deco characters, but perhaps the apotheosis in glass of the Jazz Age was the set of drawn glass figures designed by Léon Zack

for the Atelier Primavera, the interior decorating department of the Parisian store Printemps. It represented the performers of the Revue Nègre, a band of writhing musicians and a line of high-kicking chorus girls dressed only in feather boas draped loosely round their midriffs.

'Le Verre Français' cameo vase by Schneider
Height: 31.2cm
Morty & Anita, V14/15 Antiquarius, London
Price: £850

31

Object	Quality of manufacture	Quality of design and/or decoration	Rarity	Price (£)	Price ($)
Anon.					
moulded scent bottle	2	4	■	15-50	30-80
scent bottle, enamelled geom. dec.	3	6	■	40-120	60-200
decanter, enamelled geom. dec.	3	6	■	75-150	120-240
6 glasses, enamelled geom. dec.	3	6	■ ■	150-300	240-480
Baccarat					
scent bottle, enamelled	7	6	■ ■	100-250	160-400
drinking glass	7	7	■ ■	40-120	60-200
Cappellin					
vase, designed V.Zecchin	8	8	■ ■ ■	150-300	240-480
Daum					
internally decorated vase	8	7	■ ■	ʒ 300-600	480-1000
vase/bowl, acid-etched geom. dec.	8	7	■ ■	250-750	400-1200
D'Avesn					
moulded vase/bowl	7	6	■ ■ ■	200-400	320-640
Etling					
opalescent figure	6	6	■ ■ ■	400-800	640-1280
moulded vase/bowl	6	7	■ ■ ■	300-600	480-1000
Goupy, Marcel					
vase/bowl, enamelled decoration	7	8	■ ■ ■	600-1000+	1000-1600+
vase/bowl, engraved decoration	7	8	■ ■ ■	700-1000+	1120-1600+
Hunebelle					
vase/bowl, moulded	7	8	■ ■ ■	300-600	480-1000

Qualities on a scale 1-10   ■ Rare   ■ ■ Very rare   ■ ■ ■ Extremely rare

Object	Quality of manufacture	Quality of design and/or decoration	Rarity	Price (£)	Price ($)
Lalique					
ashtray, 'Souris'	8	5	■ ■	150-250	240-400
scent bottle, 'Le Parisien'	8	8	■ ■	200-250	320-400
dish, 'Ondine ouverte'	8	7	■ ■	300-400	480-640
vase, 'Soucis'	8	8	■ ■	450-550	720-880
clock-case, 'Inséparables'	8	6	■ ■	450-750	720-1200
Legras					
vase, etched/etched and enamelled	6	7	■ ■	250-500	400-800
Luce, Jean					
vase/bowl	7	8	■ ■ ■	500-1000+	800-1600+
Muller Frères					
moulded lampshade/bowl/vase	5	7	■ ■ ■	250-400	400-640
Navarre, Henri					
vase/bottle	9	8	■ ■ ■	650-1000+	1040-1600+
Orrefors					
vase/bowl/decanter	8	7	■ ■	250-600	400-1000
Robj					
moulded lampshade	6	7	■ ■ ■	300-500	480-800
Sabino					
moulded vase/bowl/lampshade	7	7	■ ■	250-450	400-720
Schneider					
vase/bowl, internally decorated	8	7	■ ■	150-400	240-640
'Charder' or 'Le Verre Français' vase/bowl, cameo decoration	8	7	■ ■	300-800	480-1280
Süe et Mare					
scent bottles (set of 3)	8	8	■ ■ ■	500-600	800-1000
Thuret, André					
vase/bottle	9	8	■ ■ ■	650-1000+	1040-1000+

Qualities on a scale 1-10   ■ Rare   ■ ■ Very rare   ■ ■ ■ Extremely rare

CHAPTER TWO

POTTERY
AND
PORCELAIN

Newport Pottery painted jug by
Clarice Cliff. Galia Antiques, Q4/5
Antiquarius, London. Price: £750.

Royal Doulton 'Tango'
porcelain coffee set
Height (coffee pot): 20.7cm
Sold: Phillips, London, 23/10/86
Price (27 pieces): £242

The fluctuating economic fortunes of the industrialized nations between the Wars led to intense competition for a share of the market, and manufacturers were forever trying to attract customers, whose affluence often dwindled as production mounted. This meant that a plethora of different styles were used to shape and decorate objects of the twenties and thirties, particularly ceramics. Most ceramics of this time are today labelled 'Art Deco'; they range from the perennial willow pattern (stylized to accord with contemporary *chinoiseries*) to the modern, geometrical designs inspired by Cubism and the Bauhaus. But although the newly invented tunnel-kiln and spray-gun increased output, rationalization of production was sometimes sacrificed to the need to lure customers from other manufacturers' lines. As a result tableware from the twenties

and thirties is found with hand-painted as well as sprayed or printed decoration. Different glaze effects were tried, too, from a crackled white used by several European manufacturers to the bright, synthetic colours of much American china.

Along with the numerous different styles and techniques used by the manufacturers, there were also many different modes of production, from the big firms like Villeroy & Boch, Haviland and Wedgwood to the individual artists who performed every process by hand. In between was a range of workshops and studios which took more or less advantage of technical innovations, usually according to the state of their finances rather than in deference to the dictates of any artistic philosophy. But whether industrial giant or artist potter, most manufacturers varied the type and style of their product in order to tempt the consumer, whose taste was as changeable as the economic climate. Novelty was an essential. A china liqueur flask in the shape of Napoleon is as Art Deco an object as a plate decorated with an abstract, geometrical design.

ENGLISH CERAMICS

To many collectors Clarice Cliff is virtually synonymous with Art Deco. Working for A.J. Wilkinson Ltd and its subsidiary, the Newport Pottery Co. Ltd, Clarice Cliff not only painted pieces herself, she also created several decorative designs which were painted by others. Under her art direction, Wilkinson commissioned outside artists, including Vanessa Bell, Duncan Grant, Laura Knight, Paul Nash, Ernest Procter and Gordon Forsyth to supply designs for decoration. There were many different lines manufactured which bear Clarice Cliff's facsimile signature; they were given names such as 'Biarritz', 'Bizarre' and 'Fantasque'. The decoration ranged from stylized versions of such traditional themes as cottages in a landscape, or flowers, to abstract geometrical designs; shapes, too, ranged from traditional to Modernist. The predominating colours were the currently fashionable orange, yellow and black.

Single pieces of Clarice Cliff's pottery sometimes fetch very high prices if the quality of the design or decoration is particularly good, and sets of tableware are also generally expensive, but so prolific was production that odd pieces of the same design can be accumulated with a little patience and at no great cost. Recently, a number of fakes have appeared on the market, and reproductions are now being manufac-

tured in Staffordshire. The latter are clearly marked as such, but the former bear facsimile marks of the original wares. The forgeries are detectable both in the quality of the painting and in the clay body used, but only to someone who has seen and handled plenty of Clarice Cliff pottery.

Susie Cooper worked for A.E. Gray & Co. from about 1925 to 1930, and then set up her own pottery in Burslem, Staffordshire, where she designed wares which were painted by herself and a team of decorators. The

Fielding 'Crown Devon' vase
Height: 25.5cm
Sold: Sotheby's, London, 16/5/86
Price: £308

37

Shelley tea set with painted decoration
Height (jug): 6cm
Sold: Christie's South Kensington, London, 25/7/86
Price (21 pieces): £420

Vase by Susie Cooper, sgraffito decoration
Height: 29cm
Margaret Knight, London
Price: £110

china she produced is today usually cheaper than Clarice Cliff's, although the designs are similar and often more sophisticated.

The success of Clarice Cliff and Susie Cooper induced other firms to produce tableware and vases decorated in bright colours with Art Deco designs. Among them were Worcester Royal Porcelain, Wiltshaw & Robinson ('Carlton' ware), Fielding ('Crown Devon'), Doulton ('Wynn', 'Tango', 'Casino', 'Merryweather' and, designed by the artist Frank Bragwyn, 'Harvest'), Bourne ('Danesby') and the Shelley Pottery ('Vogue'). In the 1930s the painter Paul Nash designed tableware decoration for

Foley. Charlotte Rhead, working for Burgess & Leigh Ltd until 1932 and then for A.G. Richardson and Co. ('Crown Ducal'), designed china in the Art Deco style. It was decorated using the tube-line process made popular by William Moorcroft, who also produced some Art Deco pottery, notably the 'Hazeldene', 'Claremont' and 'Yacht' patterns.

The hand-painted china manufactured by Wedgwood between the Wars was largely in the Arts and Crafts style rather than Art Deco, but some of the decoration designed by Millicent Taplin, Victor Skellern and Harry Trethowan during the 1920s and 1930s had a contemporary flavour. Then, in 1932, the firm commissioned the architect and designer Keith Murray to provide a range of vases and useful wares in Modernist shapes. These were produced in white, pale yellow and green glazes; some pieces were dark brown or black basalt ware, and these are more keenly collected. Between 1936 and 1940, the artist and illustrator Eric Ravilious supplied Wedgwood

with a number of decorative designs for printing on tableware.

EUROPEAN DESIGNS

French tableware decorated in the Art Deco style was usually made of porcelain. Among the more famous artists who designed decoration were Robert Bonfils, Henri Rapin, Jean Dupas and Marcel Goupy for Sèvres, Jean Dufy (Raoul's brother) for the Limoges firm of Haviland, and Suzanne Lalique (René's daughter) for both Haviland and Sèvres. Georges Rouard's gallery in Paris sold tableware decorated with designs by several artists including Marcel Goupy, and Jean Luce ran a boutique where he sold both china and glassware decorated with his own designs.

> **Foley tea set designed by Paul Nash**
> Diameter (large plate): 23cm
> Sold: Phillips, London, 13/3/86
> Price: £330

**Goldscheider group after a
model by J. Lorenzl**
Height: 43.2cm
Sold: Christie's South Kensington,
London, 19/9/86
Price: £638

Primavera, the design studio of the Printemps department store in Paris, sold a wide range of ceramics manufactured at Primavera's own factory near Tours and decorated by Claude Lévy and Mme Chauchet-Guillère among others. Most of the vases and tableware sold at La Maîtrise, the Galeries Lafayette's equivalent to Primavera, were designed by its director Maurice Dufrêne. Robj, a firm of retailers in the rue de Paradis, Paris, sold tea and dinner services which were Modernist in style, often decorated with abstract, geometrical designs.

Large quantities of German tableware were decorated during the late 1920s and early 1930s with designs inspired by Bauhaus constructivism. Shapes ranged from traditional to modern; some jugs and coffee pots, in particular, were Bauhaus shapes modified only slightly. The abstract, geometrical decoration was usually applied with stencil and spray-gun. In the larger factories two hundred items an hour could be decorated using this technique. The principal manufacturers were Villeroy & Boch, Christian Carstens, C.A. Lehmann & Son, and several potteries in Bunzlau, Silesia. The Bauhaus-trained Marguerite Friedlander designed a tea set for the State Porcelain Factory in Berlin, and in 1934 Wilhelm Wagenfeld, who had been director of the Bauhaus metalwork department, created a range of tableware for the Furstenberg porcelain factory.

The Italian artist Gio Ponti supplied designs for shapes and decoration to the porcelain manufacturers Richard-Ginori of Doccia between 1923 and 1938. Ponti's shapes were generally simple and his decoration either incorporated figures or used geometrical patterns to create *trompe l'oeil* perspectives. For the Gustavsberg factory in Sweden, Wilhelm Kåge designed a range of vases, boxes and tableware covered in a green glaze inlaid with Art Deco motifs in silver. Kåge's 'Pyro' and 'Praktika' lines of tableware and ovenware were uncompromisingly functional in their forms and austere in their decoration.

AMERICAN CERAMICS

During the 1930s, the American ceramics industry at last began to react to contemporary styles. Walter

Dorwin Teague designed the 'Conversation' line for Taylor, Smith & Taylor, and the Steubenville Potteries produced the 'American Modern' range designed by Russel Wright. He combined traditional shapes with streamlining, the current craze in the USA. In 1936 the Homer Laughlin Company introduced 'Fiesta', designed by the firm's art director Frederick H. Rhead (Charlotte's older brother who had emigrated to the USA at the turn of the century). 'Fiesta' was Modernist both in its simple forms and in its brightly coloured glazes. The Roseville Pottery Company produced the 'Futura' range of vases in a style influenced by skyscraper architecture.

CHINA FIGURES

In every specialist dealer's shop, in every antiques market, at every auction sale of twentieth-century decorative arts, and even in many junk shops, there is usually at least one Art Deco china figurine. Most typical is the model of a lissom girl, more or less décolletée, very often wearing trousers or shorts, sometimes accompanied by a greyhound or a borzoi. Her air is coquettish or languid – or both; an achievement of the twenties was a subtle combination of the two moods.

Many Art Deco figurines seem to have stepped straight from the pages of the Parisian fashion magazines. They wear evening-gowns, smart suits, négligés, bathing costumes, but, whatever their garments, they are dressed in contemporary fashion. To display the maker's ceramic virtuosity, some figurines are given broad-brimmed hats, flying scarves or frilled dresses. Nudity is quite common, although often the undressed lady

Lenci figure
Height: 51.75cm
Sold: Sotheby's, London, 16/5/86
Price: £825

41

carries a length of elegantly draped material patterned with an Art Deco design. Some of these china ladies reflect the twenties craze for costume-balls and *bals masqués*; they are dressed as clowns, Columbines and Pierrettes, or they wear the costumes of Flamenco dancers.

A great number of these female figurines are unmarked or bear only an impressed model number. Others have the modeller's signature but no factory mark. This is the case with a large proportion of the figures made in France. Very often the signature is that of an otherwise unrecorded artist.

Three sculptors of considerable merit whose signed work is not too rare were Marcel Renard, Léon Leyritz and Emile Bachelet. Renard's figures were manufactured by Primavera, Leyritz's by Fau & Guillard and Bachelet's by the Mougin brothers at Lunéville. Figures by Edouard Cazaux and Sybille May were distributed by Goldscheider of Paris. The work of all these French modellers was stylized, echoing many of the characteristics of contemporary painting and sculpture in Paris.

Outside France, Art Deco china figures were manufactured by numerous firms in many countries. The Royal Dux porcelain works in Czechoslovakia produced figures, making a speciality of Near Eastern dancers. Josef Lorenzl modelled several of the countless figures produced by Goldscheider of Vienna; another Goldscheider modeller was Walter Bosse, who also manufactured figures at his own workshop in Kufstein. Figures modelled by artists of the Wiener Werkstätte – most notably by Susi Singer and Vally Wieselthier – were made at their own

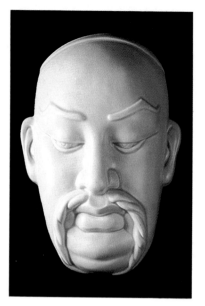

Beswick wall mask
Height: 23.2cm
Margaret Knight, London
Price: £110

ceramic workshop and at Wiener Keramik. German firms producing figures included Rosenthal, Schwartzburger, Hutschenreuther, Katzhütte, and the Berlin and Nymphenburg porcelain factories. In Italy, figures of young girls, often nude and sometimes given a rather sensuous candour, were produced by the Lenci workshops in Turin. Francesco Nonni, working in Faenza, created many stylish figures, some of them portraits of theatrical personalities. Elegant figures, often in Oriental costumes, were modelled by Arno Malinowsky for the Royal Copenhagen Porcelain Factory. In the USA the Cowan Pottery Studio produced Art

42

Deco figures modelled by Waylande Gregory and others.

Few pottery or porcelain figures made in England can properly be called Art Deco. Charles Vyse, Harry Parr, Harold and Phoebe Stabler, Eric Bradbury and Gwendoline Parnell worked in an Arts and Crafts manner, although their figures have a strong twenties flavour, and S. Nicholson-Babb made several very stylish figures in white-glazed earthenware. In the 1930s William Ruscoe made some rolled-clay figures which are, however, very rare.

Further typical subjects of Art Deco figure modelling are sportsmen and sportswomen – often playing golf or tennis, two games which grew rapidly in popularity during the twenties. Wedgwood produced a series of four athletes modelled by the sculptor Alan Best. Jazz musicians, nearly always black, reflect another contemporary craze; examples were manufactured in France by Robj and in England by A.J. Wilkinson (designed by Clarice Cliff).

Many Art Deco figures were modelled in a style of caricature, and there is a strong humorous element in them. Particularly attractive are a series of caricatures modelled by the cartoonist and poster-artist John Hassall; these have adjustable heads, to heighten the comic effect, and include a policeman, a Guardsman, a country yokel, a boy-scout and a cook.

A category of ceramic sculpture which is almost exclusively characteristic of Art Deco is the wall-mask – a face made to be hung like a picture on the wall. The colouring of these masks often reflects the contemporary fashion in make-up, and the hair is usually styled à la mode. A large number of these, unmarked and

of poor quality, were manufactured in Austria and Czechoslovakia. Others were made by Goldscheider and Bosse (Austria), Clarice Cliff and Beswick (UK) and Lenci (Italy).

ANIMALS

Animals have been one of the ceramic modeller's favourite subjects in every age and style, and Art Deco is no exception. Deer and greyhounds were particularly favoured for the elegance of their limbs. The Berlin and Sèvres porcelain factories both produced animal figures in the Art Deco style. Other notable examples are those designed by Jean-

Robj porcelain liqueur flasks
Height (taller): 21.5cm
Galia Antiques, Q4/5 Antiquarius, London
Price: £260 (left), £110 (right)

Jacques Adnet for Primavera and the animals modelled in the 'Cubist' style by the sculptor John Skeaping for Wedgwood. Also made by Wedgwood were figures of a mandarin duck and a panther modelled in a more sophisticated – nearly Cubist – manner by Alan Best, but these are much rarer.

Knud Kyhn modelled a number of animal figures which were manufactured in stoneware by Royal Copenhagen, but these are too naturalistic to be properly described as Art Deco.

The Cowan Pottery Studio produced several figures of animals and birds, many of them treated in a Cubist-orientated style; A. Drexel Jacobson was the artist responsible for most of these.

FUNCTIONAL CERAMICS

One type of ceramic which was particularly popular during the Art Deco years was useful china, such as teapots, bottles, posy-holders etc., modelled as figures, either human or animal, and sometimes in the shape of objects. Vases, bottles and boxes occur in the form of dice; their cubic shape reflects the contemporary obsession with avant-garde art. One of the most celebrated items of Art Deco is the cube tea set, which was manufactured in silver and other metals as well as in china. Other pieces which are generally easy to find are the teapots modelled as sports-cars and aeroplanes, where the driver's or pilot's head forms the handle to the lid. In America, the Hall China Company even produced teapots shaped as footballs, doughnuts and automobiles. A much rarer variation on this theme is the teapot in the form of a streamlined railway engine. Haviland produced a tea set in the form of various birds and animals, modelled by Edouard-Marcel Sandoz, and Mabel Lucie Attwell designed a tea set for Shelley, each piece in the shape of a different comic animal. Walt Disney characters appeared as the pieces of a tea set made by Wadeheath (England).

The French firm of Robj produced, during the twenties, a series of china liqueur bottles in the forms of a Turk,

Goldscheider wall mask
Height: 34.5cm
Sold: Sotheby's, London, 16/5/86
Price: £286

**China figures designed
by John Hassall**
Height (tallest): 15.5cm
Sold: Christie's South Kensington,
London, 25/7/86
Price: £150

a Chinaman, a Scotsman, a Dutchman, a black cook, a monk, Napoleon, a girl carrying a basket of flowers, and other figures; in each case the head forms the stopper. The same firm made numerous china bookends modelled as clowns, Pierrots, Red Indians in canoes etc., and the figurative bookend was widely manufactured during the period. The English artist Louis Wain was commissioned by an unknown manufacturer to model vases in the form of 'Cubist' cats and dogs. There are many other examples of the genre, and this menagerie of useful china can be a whole area of specialization for the collector in itself.

DECORATION TECHNIQUES

Most Art Deco figures are brightly coloured in the popular hues of the twenties — tango-orange, peppermint-green, red, yellow, turquoise and black. But many are covered with a white or cream-coloured crackled glaze, sometimes with touches of contrasting colour such as a red rose or a black mask. This treatment was used for a wide range of Art Deco ceramics, apart from figures.

By the 1920s electric kilns were widely used, and the precise control of the rate of cooling facilitated the achievement of crackled glazes. The results appealed to contemporary

45

**Boch 'Keramis' stoneware
vase by Charles Catteau**
Height: 27.8cm
Malcolm Haslam, London
Price: £300

have decoration thickly applied in bright colours. The decoration of the Carter Stabler Adams version is painted over the glaze, the crackle of which is usually less pronounced than the Belgian and French wares. All three factories used animal and floral decorative motifs, sometimes human figures, always stylized and arranged in formal bands; alternatively, the decoration is abstract and geometric. Examples of all three of these firms' wares are comparatively common, and comparatively inexpensive. Much rarer is the tableware produced by the Compagnie des Artistes Français, most of which was also covered in a crackled white glaze. A similar technique was used on anonymous figures of deer, doves, greyhounds, clowns, ladies etc., but these are easier to find because they were made in such profusion.

**Carter, Stabler & Adams
painted tile designed
by Edward Bawden**
15 x 15cm
Malcolm Haslam, London
Price: £50

taste, which also appreciated the random decorative effects of wood-grain and marble. Very often the crackled glaze was used as a ground for a painted or enamelled decorative design.

Three factories in particular produced this sort of ware: Boch Frères (Belgium), Longwy (France), and Carter Stabler Adams (England), whose ceramics are sometimes known as Poole. Boch Frères called theirs 'Keramis' and many pieces bear the facsimile signature of Charles Catteau, who designed much of the decoration. Longwy made a similar type of pottery for Primavera, and this name is often painted on the base. 'Keramis' and Longwy wares

STUDIO-POTTERS

Before the First World War there had been only a handful of artist-potters in Europe and America, but during the 1930s they added a new dimension to decorative ceramics. Work by the best of them was exhibited in art galleries and commanded high prices. Connoisseurs began to collect pottery as well as pictures and sculptures. Often, the studio-potters were more concerned with general aesthetic theories than the decorative style of the day. In consequence, much of the studio-pottery of the Art Deco era has less to do with Art Deco than with, for example, ancient Chinese or Sung ceramics. In England, only William Staite Murray, Katharine Pleydell-Bouverie and Charles Vyse among the leading studio-potters occasionally used Art Deco motifs to decorate their otherwise Sung-inspired pots.

In France, where contemporary

Stoneware vase by Katharine Pleydell-Bouverie
Height: 7.5cm
Malcolm Haslam, London
Price: £650

style has always tended to be more of an imperative than elsewhere, the studio-potters incorporated Art Deco motifs in their work to a considerable extent. Raoul Lachenal and Henri Simmen both made stoneware decorated with geometrical Art Deco designs. Emile Decœur and Emile Lenoble used floral and geometric decoration treated in an Art Deco manner. Some other French studio-potters, most notably René Buthaud, painted their pots in the style of the Ecole de Paris, from which so much of Art Deco was derived. Lallemant not only painted his china with Art Deco designs, but he also made it in Art Deco shapes. From his workshop

Shelley tea set designed by Mabel Lucy Attwell
Height (teapot): 13.5cm
Sold: Phillips, London, 6/2/86
Price: £330

emanated a range of bottles and vases painted with a wide variety of subjects, often with a title or a line of verse incorporated in the design. Sporting and nursery themes were typical.

In the USA, some studio-potters were inspired by American Indian art or Modernism to make ceramics which can be described as Art Deco. Both influences are evident in the work of Maija Grotell and some members of the Cowan Pottery Studio. Victor Schreckengost, who worked at the Cowan Pottery Studio until it went out of business in 1931, made porcelain vessels decorated with Art

Deco designs. These are rare and expensive, as are the plates and bowls made and painted by Henry Varnum Poor and Wilhelm Hunt Diederich. Poor turned to ceramics

first made, many pieces now fetch high — sometimes exorbitant — prices, quite out of proportion to their quality or rarity. Figures often reflect the fashions and styles of the twenties and thirties, particularly the girls, and many have all the élan and camp of the period. Crackled white or cream glazed wares are perhaps the most authentic Art Deco ceramics, and are generally less expensive than other hand-painted wares. Studio-pottery is less essentially Art Deco in style, but it is often good value, considering that each piece is unique.

in 1920 when he found that his paintings did not sell. He decorated his pottery with figurative designs in the style of the Ecole de Paris. Diederich worked primarily in bronze, but produced ceramics for a short period during the 1920s. He painted his pottery with the same sporting and animal designs which he used for his metalwork.

Although pottery and porcelain by American studio-potters is rare and tends to be very expensive, there can be little doubt that much of it still remains to be found; for example, the original 'Jazz Bowl' made by Schrec-kengost in 1931, inspired by an evening spent at the Cotton Club in New York. The bowl was such a success that he made a total of fifty examples, all slightly different. But today the whereabouts of only a few of them are known.

COLLECTING CERAMICS

Although much of the Art Deco ceramics were cheap when they were

Fraureuth porcelain box and cover
Height: 18.5cm
Sold: Sotheby's, London, 16/5/86
Price: £418

49

Object	Quality of manufacture	Quality of design and/or decoration	Rarity	Price (£)	Price ($)
Anon.					
wall mask	4	6	■	20-100	40-160
figure	2	6	■	20-40	40-60
figure	4	6	■	40-80	60-130
Baudisch, Gudrun					
figure	7	8	■ ■ ■	800-1000	1280-1600
Berlin					
figure, G.Schliepstein	8	8	■ ■	300-500	480-800
Boch Frères					
'Keramis' vase	7	7	■ ■	100-200	160-320
'Grès Keramis' stoneware vase	8	7	■ ■ ■	150-300	240-480
'Keramis' vase, C.Catteau	7	8	■ ■ ■	120-240	200-380
'Grès Keramis' vase, C.Catteau	8	8	■ ■ ■	175-400	280-640
Carter Stabler Adams					
tile, painted	7	8	■ ■	25-50	45-80
vase/bowl/dish, painted decoration	7	8	■	40-120	60-200
Cliff, Clarice					
vase/jug	5	6	■	150-300	240-480
vase, 'Yoyo' or other unusual geometrical shape or decoration	5	7	■ ■	300-600	480-1000
vase, 'Inspiration'	5	7	■ ■	400-800	640-1280
wall mask	5	6	■ ■ ■	300-600	480-1000
Copenhagen					
porcelain figure, A.Malinowski	9	7	■ ■	300-500	480-800
stoneware figure, K.Kyn	9	6	■ ■	500-750	800-1200
Cooper, Susie					
coffee/tea set (15 pieces), painted	5	7	■ ■	150-250	240-400

Qualities on a scale 1-10   ■ Rare   ■ ■ Very rare   ■ ■ ■ Extremely rare

Object	Quality of manufacture	Quality of design and/or decoration	Rarity	Price (£)	Price ($)
Cooper, Susie contd					
vase/bowl, painted decoration	5	7	■	50-150	80-240
vase, relief decoration	5	7	■ ■	75-200	120-320
Doulton					
'Tango' coffee set (20 pieces)	6	7	■ ■ ■	200-250	320-400
'Casino' tea set (8 pieces)	6	7	■ ■ ■	100-200	160-320
'Merryweather' coffee/tea set (12 pieces)	6	6	■	50-100	80-160
'Sweet Anne' wall mask	6	5	■ ■	200-300	320-480
Fielding					
'Crown Devon' vase/bowl, painted	6	6	■	50-150	80-240
'Crown Devon' vase, stylish shape/ decoration	6	8	■ ■ ■	150-300	240-480
Foley					
tea set (18 pieces), designed Paul Nash	6	8	■ ■ ■	250-350	400-560
Goldscheider					
vase/bowl	7	7	■ ■	60-120	100-200
figure	7	7	■ ■	100-300	160-320
figure, J.Lorenzl	7	8	■ ■	400-600	640-1000
wall mask	7	7	■ ■	150-300	240-480
Homer Laughlin					
jug/bowl, 'Fiesta', F.Rhead	5	7	■ ■	50-120	80-200
Lallemant					
vase, painted decoration	8	8	■ ■ ■	250-500	400-800
Lenci					
figure	8	7	■ ■	200-400	320-640
figure, bizarre/risqué	8	7	■ ■	600-1000+	1000-1600+

Qualities on a scale 1-10   ■ Rare   ■ ■ Very rare   ■ ■ ■ Extremely rare   51

Object	Quality of manufacture	Quality of design and/or decoration	Rarity	Price (£)	Price ($)
Lenoble, Emile					
stoneware vase/bowl	10	9	■ ■ ■	800-1000+	1280-1600+
Leyritz, Léon					
figure	7	8	■ ■	75-150	120-240
Parr, Harry					
figure	8	7	■ ■	150-300	240-480
Rhead, Charlotte					
dish 'Manchu'	6	7	■ ■	100-200	160-320
dish 'Persian'	6	7	■ ■	150-300	240-480
Robj					
figural flask	6	8	■ ■	120-240	200-380
Rosenthal					
figure	9	8	■ ■	500-1000+	800-1600+
Roseville					
'Futura' vase	3	6	■ ■	80-160	130-260
Royal Dux					
figure	7	7	■ ■	150-350	240-560
Schwartzburger					
figure, M.Pfeiffer	7	7	■ ■	150-250	240-400
figure, G.Schliepstein	7	8	■ ■	200-400	320-640
figure, H.Meisel	7	8	■ ■	300-450	480-720
Sèvres					
vase, painted decoration	9	8	■ ■	200-400	320-640
vase, painted and pate-sur-pate	10	8	■ ■ ■	450-750	720-1200

Qualities on a scale 1-10   ■ Rare   ■ ■ Very rare   ■ ■ ■ Extremely rare

Object	Quality of manufacture	Quality of design and/or decoration	Rarity	Price (£)	Price ($)
Shelley					
tea set (20 pieces), geometrical dec.	5	6	■	400-500	640-800
tea set (20 pieces), stylized landscape pattern	5	5	■	50-100	80-160
tea set (3 pieces), 'elfin', M.L.Attwell	5	6	■ ■	150-200	240-320
tea set (3 pieces), animals, M.L.Attwell	5	7	■ ■	250-350	400-560
figure, golfer, M.L.Attwell	5	7	■ ■ ■	275-350	440-560
Steubenville					
jug/bowl, 'American Modern', R.Wright	6	9	■ ■	120-240	200-380
Taylor, Smith & Taylor					
jug/bowl, 'Conversation', W.Teague	5	8	■ ■	100-200	160-320
Vyse, Charles					
figure	9	7	■ ■	300-500	480-800
vase/bowl, stoneware	9	7	■ ■	150-350	240-560
Wedgwood					
vase/bowl, K.Murray	7	8	■	50-120	80-200
vase/bowl black/brown basalt, K.Murray	8	8	■ ■ ■	100-200	160-320
animal figure, J.Skeaping	7	7	■ ■	100-250	160-400
animal figure, A.Best	7	8	■ ■ ■	200-400	320-640
athlete figure, A.Best	7	6	■ ■ ■	150-300	240-480

Qualities on a scale 1-10   ■ Rare   ■ ■ Very rare   ■ ■ ■ Extremely rare   53

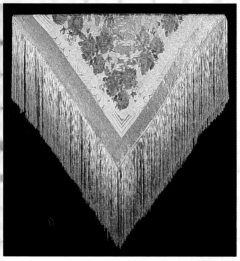

CHAPTER THREE

FASHION AND ACCESSORIES

Shawl in woven silk and metal thread.
Cornucopia, London. Price: £175.

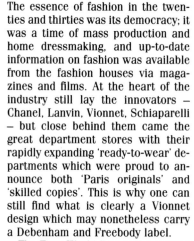

Coat with net inserts
Length: 130cm
Cornucopia, London
Price: £50

The essence of fashion in the twenties and thirties was its democracy; it was a time of mass production and home dressmaking, and up-to-date information on fashion was available from the fashion houses via magazines and films. At the heart of the industry still lay the innovators – Chanel, Lanvin, Vionnet, Schiaparelli – but close behind them came the great department stores with their rapidly expanding 'ready-to-wear' departments which were proud to announce both 'Paris originals' and 'skilled copies'. This is why one can still find what is clearly a Vionnet design which may nonetheless carry a Debenham and Freebody label.

The First World War had a radical effect on fashion, not simply because more women were working and needed clothing which was relatively easy to wear, but because in the end a much wider social range of women were working and earning money of their own; this fact alone contributed a great deal to the emergence of 'the new woman' whose existence Coco Chanel was so quick to recognize. At the height of her success as a couturier Chanel remarked, 'Fashion does not exist unless it goes down into the streets.' In many ways this apparently simple statement sums up the world of difference between the fashions of the period from 1900 to 1914 and those of the twenties and thirties. With her usual perspicacity Chanel made clothes for 'the new woman' and although her original designs were expensive her clients were paying for her ideas rather than costly materials or impossibly intricate cut. Between the Wars couture clothing remained the prerogative of the rich but *fashion* did not. Perhaps relatively few women could buy a Chanel original, but anyone who wished could copy her ideas and wear something which was immediately chic.

The clothing industry was also quick to realize the potential of the new market and of the designs coming from Paris. Off-the-peg garments had been available since the mid-nineteenth century but the complexity of fashionable tailoring then made the production of such garments in a wide range of sizes an economic impossibility. Usually, so-called ready-to-wear garments were anything but because they were sold only partly finished so that the final tailoring could be done at home or else in the store's own finishing department. The new unstructured clothes which began to appear by the early twenties lent themselves easily to mass manufacture; because 'fit' in the nineteenth-century sense of the word was no longer a consideration, store-bought clothes could be altered simply, and in any case, by the mid-twenties the range of sizes produced by dress manufacturers had increased so that alteration was often not necessary.

The paper pattern industry, which had been in existence since the mid-nineteenth century, also benefited from the new simplicity in style, and established companies such as Butterick and Weldon found themselves with a rapidly expanding market. The final contributing factor to the spread of fashion across a wide social range was the introduction in the mid-twenties of rayon, which looked and felt like silk; it made a passable imitation of that most exclusive of fabrics available to almost anyone.

The most innovative of the pre-War designers, Paul Poiret, regarded all these developments with some displeasure; to him they represented a

Evening dress in silk georgette and net
Length: 160cm
Cornucopia, London
Price: £85

betrayal of everything that fashion should be. To Poiret, Chanel was not a couturier (and certainly in the old sense of the word she was not), but what he failed to see was the growing importance of the designer as a source of ideas. In the twenties couturiers still retained their exclusive clientele – smart women from Europe and America still preferred to be dressed in Paris. But increasingly the fashion collections were a source of ideas and inspiration to a much wider buying public. In the economic depression of the thirties, when the old couture market no longer existed, the mass production of fashion assumed a role of great importance in the success or failure of the fashion houses.

CHANEL

It was undoubtedly Chanel who pulled together the elements which we now regard as typical of twenties fashion. It was she who, during the First World War, first adapted men's suits and sweaters, and sailors' jackets, for women. The line she evolved then, bypassing the waist and dropping the seamline to the hip, continued after the War in the dresses and suits she designed for her fashion house in Paris. Her ideas came less from the traditional concepts of fashion than from sportswear; the classic Chanel suit is a modified cardigan teamed with a matching skirt. Her fabrics were equally unex-

---

Crêpe wrap embroidered in silk
Length: 130cm
Cornucopia, London
Price: £50

Evening jacket, net embroidered with sequins
Length: 45cm
Cornucopia, London
Price: £50

element lying in the fact that the dress, or more usually the cardigan, would be beautifully beaded.

In America Chanel's influence was enormous; wholesalers from the United States were buying her clothes from the early twenties and copies of her suits were available at every level of fashion mass production. Her visit to Hollywood in the early twenties influenced costume design in the cinema, which gave her ideas probably the widest audience enjoyed by any designer to that date. The basic themes of Chanel's designs changed very little over the two decades between the Wars; there were variations in skirt length and infinite variety in the detailing, but the notion of the fashion 'classic' originates with her. Her continued success throughout the thirties when Paris

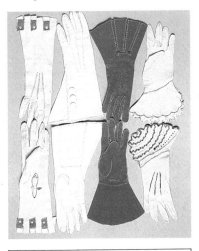

Gauntlet gloves in suede and leather
Length: 30cm
Cornucopia, London
Price (per pair): £20

pected – flannel and wool jersey which had been used previously for utilitarian clothes or else for sensible undergarments were exploited for their fluidity and ease of wearing. She said, 'I make fashions women can live in, breathe in, feel comfortable in and look younger in.' These were not ideas which had occupied designers before the war.

Chanel's revolutionary approach to couture extended to jewellery. She liked costume jewellery which was obviously fake, huge rows of randomly sized glass beads and ropes of impossibly large pearls. Her evening wear, too, was a deliberate contradiction; straight dresses teamed with a cardigan jacket, the surprise

59

couture was undergoing its worst years, falling from second to twenty-seventh place in France's export market, is in part due to the versatility of her designs.

JEAN PATOU

Like Chanel, Jean Patou understood the need for the designers to approach the mass market on their own terms. He too achieved considerable success in America with clothes that were simple and fluid, designed for a slim, boyish figure. Like Molyneux, who began his career in the twenties, Patou evolved an important addition to womens' fashion. The tailor-made or tailored suit had first appeared in the late nineteenth century but was considered to be sportswear, suitable only for walking, golfing or shooting. Patou and Molyneux recognized the potential of the suit for the new professional woman or for the woman who wished to express her independence in her clothing as she did in her lifestyle. The ready-to-wear suit became an important fashion item in the twenties and survived through the thirties; even today it still retains the status given to it sixty years ago by Patou and Molyneux as an indispensible outfit for the professional woman.

VIONNET

Although the prevailing line of twenties fashion minimized the breasts and hips and bypassed the waist, there were exceptions to this general rule. Towards the end of the decade there were distinct signs that designers were bored with this silhouette and with the ubiquitous short skirt, which had reached knee length in 1926 and remained there with minor

Cape in monkey fur
Length: 76cm
Cornucopia, London
Price: £250

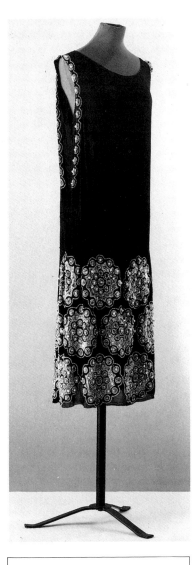

**Evening dress of silk georgette
embroidered with beads**
Length: 125cm
Cornucopia, London
Price: £150

variations. One of the first designers to offer a real alternative was Vionnet, who perfected the technique of bias cutting, of using fabric so that it clings to the body or else falls in fluid folds. In the late twenties she produced dresses in bias-cut chiffon which, while they still had a low waist also gently emphasized the breasts and hips and gave a skirt which fell in soft uneven folds. It was her designs, her use of satin and crêpe de Chine for evening dresses, and of bias-cut wool flannel for day dresses, which influenced popular fashion in the thirties. The sensuality and absolute femininity of her clothes made them a natural reference point for Hollywood designers; both Travis Banton and Adrian made clothes for stars such as Carole Lombard, Joan Crawford, Greta Garbo and Jean Harlow which were very evidently influenced by Vionnet.

SCHIAPARELLI AND OTHERS

Despite the Depression and the growing influence of the Hollywood film industry as a fashion source, Paris remained the nucleus of the fashion world in the thirties. Designers still gravitated there, and in fact many of the couturiers working from Paris were not French: Molyneux was Irish, Mainbocher American, Maggy Rouff came from Belgium, Balenciaga from Spain and Schiaparelli was Italian. Each brought their own particular ideas to the French industry and perhaps it was this diversity which helped to keep Paris couture alive. Elsa Schiaparelli, for example, was the complete antithesis to Chanel; where the latter produced clothes which were chic, comfortable and wearable, Schiaparelli made garments which were outrageous and

61

demanding. She was a skilled cutter and capable of producing garments of conventional elegance, but she chose to make clothes and accessories which effectively straddled the line between fashion and art. The Surrealist painters made fabric designs for her; she borrowed ideas from Cubism and Dada; fabrics were taken out of their traditional contexts – she used tweeds for evening clothes, turned items as tiny as buttons into sculptures, hats became shoes and handbags became musical boxes.

All this was accomplished with great style and Schiaparelli's influence on mainstream fashion was considerable. It was she who introduced the exaggerated shoulder line in 1933, an idea which reached its widest audience via the cinema, specifically in costumes designed for Joan Crawford by Adrian. She designed fabrics and clothes for Viyella

and marketed her own accessories in a boutique she opened in 1935. Outrageous as they were, Schiaparelli's ideas were a gift to mass manufacturers. The exaggerated shoulder line with its necessary padding solved one of the major problems of sizing; a woman with medium build and narrow shoulders could take the same size as a woman with medium build and wide shoulders – the padding took care of the difference. A basic dress shape could be varied with interesting detail and it is possible to find mass-produced evening dresses from the mid-thirties which are fairly conventional in their cut but which have, for example, sleeves appliquéd with cellophane strips or a bodice trimmed with small contrasting pompoms, both ideas borrowed from Schiaparelli.

THE GLAMOUR OF DECO

It is evident that fashion in the thirties had an element of escapism; both Paris and Hollywood produced garments of undeniable glamour as if in direct contradiction to the grim state of Western economy following the Wall Street crash. Furs became important for day and evening wear either in the form of a cape, a jacket, or as a scarf consisting of two skins (preferably silver fox) draped to hang at the back. Hats too were an indispensible accessory, becoming larger in direct proportion to the longer dress length and streamlined silhouette. Chanel can be credited with the introduction of lounging pyjamas in the twenties; by the mid-thirties they had evolved into beach pyjamas and from there into an acceptable item of casual wear.

Beaded, and later sequinned, dresses and jackets were an important

Hat in black velvet and fur
Diameter: 16cm
Cornucopia, London
Price: £25

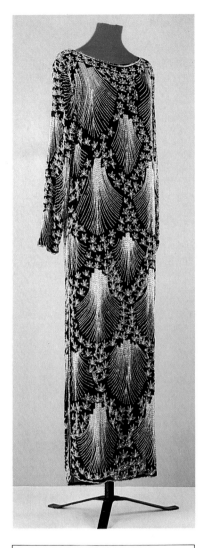

Evening dress of silk chiffon heavily embroidered with beads
Length: 170cm
Paul Rossin, London
Price: £900

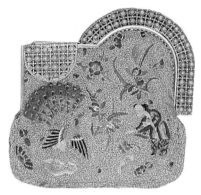

Metal framed handbag in embroidered fabric
Height: 16cm
Cornucopia, London
Price: £25

element of Art Deco fashion. The simple lines of twenties evening dresses lent themselves to the rich surfaces and elaborate patterns of hand-beading just as, in the thirties, the smooth, streamlined silhouette of the bias-cut gown was complemented by the metallic shimmer of sequins. Undoubtedly the best beaded dresses in the twenties came from France either as ready-made garments or in the form of pieces already decorated and needing only to be sewn together and lined. While the basic shape of evening dresses changed very little from year to year between 1923 and 1928, the range of patterns in beading was almost limitless. There were designs taken from Egyptian sources, from French rococo textiles, 'jazz' patterns, Oriental-inspired motifs and even designs which looked back to Art Nouveau with stylized peacocks or floral patterns.

On the more expensive garments 63

Day dress, in rayon crepe
Length: 135cm
Cornucopia, London
Price: £25

tiny beading was applied to silk chiffon to produce dresses which were extremely fragile but which had a lightness and delicacy lacking in the heavier silk crêpe versions. In less costly dresses beading was applied to rayon or cotton. Obviously, because beading was done by hand, these garments were by their very nature expensive irrespective of whether they were couture or off the peg; for those who could not afford the luxury of a completely beaded gown it was possible to buy motifs which could be appliquéd to a plain dress.

The elaborate surface decoration of the twenties was inappropriate to the sleek fashions of the thirties. Beading was still used for evening clothes but tended to be confined to jackets with dramatic geometric patterns, made to be worn over simple, undecorated frocks in the Chanel manner. On the other hand, sequins were more popular. Chanel herself made evening outfits which were completely covered with tiny metallic sequins and which are perhaps the most glamorous examples of her work and were widely copied.

FASHION FOR THE MASSES

It would obviously be untrue to claim that there is no difference between couture clothing and the clothing produced for the mass market between the Wars. A factory-made garment, manufactured with an eye to economy, is bound to be less well finished and less well detailed than one which has been individually cut and hand finished, although the finish on mass-produced garments of this period is immeasurably superior to its modern equivalent. Fashion made for the upper echelons of the mass market for stores such as Harrods, Debenham and Freebody, and Whiteley's in London, or for Macy's, Bergdorf Goodman or Lord & Taylor in America, was always of a very high quality and often finished by hand. Usually it carried the store's own label and, particularly in the United States, some indication of the size.

The mass production of fashion in Britain in the thirties was boosted by ideas from America, where techniques of manufacture were more sophisticated and where a standard sizing system had been established by the twenties. British fashion companies began importing American experts; among them Sam and Lou Krohnberg, who arrived in England in 1933 to advise the 'Peggy Page' dress company, and Jack Liss, whose 'Princess' dress company produced garments that were of a very high standard but still of a reasonable price.

Mention must also be made of the professional, or 'corner' dressmaker, once one of the mainstays of fashion and indispensable to the smart woman who could not afford to shop in Paris. Between the Wars it was still possible for a skilled tailoress to make a living by producing bespoke copies of couture clothes, although the increasing availability of chic, ready-to-wear garments posed a threat so serious that by the late 1940s the 'corner' dressmaker had all but vanished. A garment made by a good, probably store-trained, tailoress was of a very high standard with a finish comparable to that of the couture houses. The real clue to the origins of these garments lies in their detail: fastenings, bindings and so on tended to be stock items bought from a haberdashery rather than specially made.

ACCESSORIES

The accessory trade grew in proportion to the clothing industry and with a similarly wide range in price and quality. It was possible, for example, to pay fifteen guineas (about sixty-three dollars at the exchange rate at the time) for a model hat in Harrods millinery department at the beginning of the 1930s – a mass-produced hat could be bought for fifteen shillings (three dollars). Hats were an important accessory in the twenties, but they tended to have a uniform appearance. Although each designer working in the twenties made his or her own personal contribution to the overall 'look' of the decade, they all recognized that only one sort of hat was appropriate to the straight lines and shorter skirts of the new fashions; in the drawings of Chanel, Patou, Molyneux and Poiret the clothes are shown with a felt or straw cloche, the bell-shaped hat designed to be worn pulled well down over the head and which looked best over short hair. The cloche could

Leather evening shoes with marcasite buckles
Height: 10cm
Cornucopia, London
Price: £25

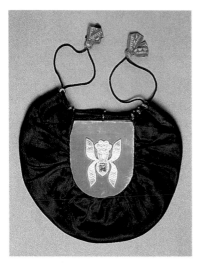

be decorated with feathers or flowers or with a simple band finished with a bow to one side, but the basic shape remained the same until the end of the decade.

In the thirties the millinery trade, free to experiment with shapes again after the restrictions of the ubiquitous cloche of the twenties, produced some extravagant fantasies, most particularly the 'Gainsborough' hat trimmed with feathers, and the tiny 'toy' hats designed to be worn well forward on the head. A handmade original, expensively trimmed and properly finished, was well beyond the budget of the average woman, but large departmental stores were stocking inexpensive smart hats just

Drawstring handbag in appliquéd silk Height: 29cm Cornucopia, London Price: £20	**'Clutch' bag in black suede and chrome** 15 x 23cm Margaret Knight, London Price: £20

Picture hat in lightweight straw
Diameter: 40cm
Cornucopia, London
Price: £25

as they were stocking inexpensive and smart clothing. The number of new millinery companies in the thirties almost equals the number of new clothing companies.

The same price range was found in the areas of footwear and gloves, both manufactured in a wide variety of materials. The round-toed, medium-heeled court shoe, which came into fashion at the end of the 1920s, was produced in reptile skin or a range of leathers, for day wear, and in coloured satins for evening. Both the shoe and glove industries benefited from the new standard sizes; a mass-produced item from the thirties will inevitably carry the size printed on the lining even if it does not bear a manufacturer's name.

Women had been using handbags from the end of the nineteenth century, when the slim silhouette of dresses made pockets almost impossible. In the twenties a fashionable woman needed a bag simply to transport the chic accessories of the period – a powder compact, a cigarette case and holder and a lipstick holder. Evening bags from the twenties are particularly interesting because they often sit on the borderline between accessory and jewellery; in fact some of the more costly and elaborate ones were actually sold through jewellery shops. Asprey, Primavera and Cartier produced exquisite purses with beaded decoration mounted on gold frames and gold chain handles set with semi-precious stones. Less costly were the mesh bags made from silver or silver plate, again with a chain handle designed to be slipped over the wrist when dancing.

The most popular shape of the thirties, and the one which best complemented the slim outline of costume, was the 'clutch', a bag designed with no handle or with an unobtrusive strap at the back, and intended to be carried tucked under the arm. The most expensive examples were made from lizard or crocodile skin worked in geometric patterns and with built-in, matching 'handbag furniture' – a purse, often mounted on a slim chain, a leather-backed mirror and a note book. Other variations were made in suede, sometimes on a chromed metal frame and with chrome initials (a monogram need not necessarily mean that a bag was a unique item, as many retailers offered a monogramming service on their more expensive bags). The same basic design appears in much cheaper handbags made from coarser leather and sometimes from leather stamped to look like reptile skin.

Perhaps the most inventive and witty designs were to be found in purses made from rigid plastic, possibly because the material was itself so 'modern' that the designers felt free to be as imaginative as they wished. Often brightly coloured, these bags carry motifs derived from sources as disparate as Modernist painting and the animated cartoon.

COLLECTING DECO FASHION

There is still tremendous scope for collectors of costume and accessories from the twenties and thirties, unless they wish to concentrate exclusively on couture. Mass production means that there are many surviving examples of very stylish dresses, shoes, gloves and bags. Hats are in shorter supply, arguably because they are difficult to store and tended to be thrown out when they became *passé*.

It is usually the most typical examples of design which find their way into shops dealing with Art Deco: beaded and sequinned dresses and jackets, for example, which are instantly identifiable and also visually spectacular; or plastic handbags. Shops which deal in 'retro' clothing (which now includes anything from the 1960s back) are good places to

**Coat in wool bouclé with
monkey fur trim**
Length: 131cm
Cornucopia, London
Price: £50

search, as are general antique shops. It is not unusual to find gloves and bags in such places even if the shop does not deal in costume. It is still worth visiting jumble sales (although the chances of finding an original Schiaparelli there are fairly remote) and it is particularly worth visiting jumble sales and thrift shops away from large cities. Anyone determined to acquire couture clothing must inevitably visit a specialist costume auction at one of the larger auction houses. On the other hand, good, non-couture clothing does turn up in general provincial auctions often as a job-lot with more modern items.

A keen collector must be prepared to see through the results of shameful mistreatment; no item of clothing is improved by being badly stored, and a crumpled rag of satin can, and gratifyingly sometimes does, turn out to be a bias-cut evening dress made in imitation of Vionnet. Unless the actual fabric has rotted most garments can be restored. Similarly, if the leather is sound, gloves, shoes and bags can be brought back to life. Hats are more of a problem; the reshaping of felt, for instance, is a skilled job and requires professional equipment. Unfortunately, unless a hat has been stored in a box and protected with tissue paper its chances of survival are low. Furs often survive because, like jewellery, they have an intrinsic value; it is still possible to find an intricately cut thirties musquash jacket among the generalized fur coats in a retro shop.

Collectors of costume from the twenties and thirties may feel themselves faced with a bewildering and apparently limitless choice; if an object is not made of precious materials and does not carry a designer's or craftsman's signature, how

Satin evening shoes
Height: 10cm
Cornucopia, London
Price: £25

can its value be judged? The answer has to be simply – on the basis of style. Clothes and accessories carry as much information about the design preoccupations between the Wars as do the furniture or ceramics or architecture. In many ways, however, costume reflects those preoccupations more accurately, because it changes from year to year in a way that furniture, for example, cannot.

There are few problems with forgeries or reproductions; to forge antique costume is simply not worthwhile. In recent years sequinned and beaded dresses made in the twenties style have been imported from the Far East, but close examination will instantly reveal that the materials are modern and the quality of finish is very inferior to the original. The same applies to retro styled dresses which were popular in England and America in the late sixties and early seventies; if you find yourself looking at polyester crêpe you may be reasonably sure that you are not looking at an original!

Object	Quality of manufacture	Quality of design and/or decoration	Rarity	Price (£)	Price ($)
Blouses					
blouse, silk satin, embroidered detail	7	7	■ ■	30-50	50-80
blouse, rayon, machine embroidery	6	6	■	10-20	20-40
blouse, lawn, embroidered detail	7	7	■ ■	30-60	50-100
Coats, jackets					
couture evening coat	8	8	■ ■ ■	900-1000+	1440-1600+
non-couture evening coat	7	8	■ ■	100-200	160-320
fox fur evening jacket	7	7	■ ■	200-300	320-480
pair of silver fox furs – evening wrap	7	7	■ ■	150-200	240-320
couture day coat	8	8	■ ■ ■	900-1000+	1440-1600+
non-couture day coat with fur trim	7	7	■ ■	75-100	120-150
Day wear					
couture day dress or suit	8	8	■ ■ ■	900-1000+	1440-1600+
non-couture day dress	6	6	■	35-50	55-80
non-couture suit	7	7	■ ■	40-60	60-100
Evening wear					
couture evening dress	8	8	■ ■ ■	900-1000+	1440-1600+
non-couture evening dress	7	7	■ ■	100-200	160-320
Gloves					
gloves, crochet	6	6	■	5-15	10-30
gloves, embroidered fabric	7	7	■ ■	10-15	20-30
gloves, leather 'gauntlet' style	7	7	■ ■	25-50	45-80
Handbags					
evening bag, on gold frame	8	8	■ ■ ■	500-700	800-1120
evening bag, on ivory frame	8	8	■ ■ ■	100-200	160-320
evening bag, on plastic frame	7	8	■ ■	75-150	120-240
evening bag, enamelled	7	8	■ ■	150-200	240-320
day handbag, leather	7	8	■ ■	30-50	50-80
day handbag, crocodile	7	8	■ ■	50-100	80-160

Qualities on a scale 1-10   ■ Rare   ■ ■ Very rare   ■ ■ ■ Extremely rare

Object	Quality of manufacture	Quality of design and/or decoration	Rarity	Price (£)	Price ($)
Knitwear					
sweater, crochet silk	7	7	■ ■	50-100	80-160
sweater, knitted wool	6	7	■ ■	20-40	40-60
Lingerie, shawls					
lingerie, satin or silk crêpe de chine	8	8	■ ■	10-50	20-80
lingerie, rayon	5	5	■	5-30	10-50
silk stockings	7	6	■ ■	5-15	10-30
kimono, silk with embroidery	7	7	■ ■	50-100	80-160
shawl, silk, heavily embroidered	8	8	■ ■	300-500	480-800
shawl, silk, with some embroidery	6	6	■	35-50	55-80
Millinery					
couture hat – cloche	8	8	■ ■ ■	200	320
non-couture felt or fine straw cloche	7	7	■ ■ ■	25-50	45-80
thirties couture hat	8	8	■ ■ ■	200-400	320-640
thirties hat – straw	7	7	■ ■	50-75	80-120
thirties hat – felt	7	7	■ ■	25-50	45-80
thirties hat – silk	7	7	■ ■	30-50	50-80
Sequinned/beaded garments					
couture evening dress	8	8	■ ■ ■	900-1000	1440-1600
couture jacket	8	8	■ ■ ■	900-1000	1440-1600
non-couture evening dress	7	7	■ ■	600-800	1000-1280
non-couture evening jacket	7	7	■ ■	150-300	240-480
evening cape	7	7	■ ■	100	160
Shoes					
evening shoes, brocade or satin	5-8	5	■ ■	20-40	40-60
day shoes, leather	7	8	■ ■	20-40	40-60
day shoes, crocodile or lizard	7	8	■ ■	25-50	45-80

Qualities on a scale 1-10   ■ Rare   ■ ■ Very rare   ■ ■ ■ Extremely rare

CHAPTER FOUR

PRINTS
AND
POSTERS

Lithographic poster by G.K. Benda.
Sold: Sotheby's, London, 16/5/86.
Price: £308.

**Pochoir print by
Charles Martin from
*Gazette du Bon Ton***
16.9 x 13.5 cm (print area)
Pruskin Gallery, London
Price: £60

On 18 December 1919 the picture-dealer René Gimpel wrote in his diary:
'Taste is entering the home in the form of advertisements. Parisians are beginning to receive extremely pretty cards, of all colours, in their mail. These ought to be kept: they'd make a picturesque collection. Ephemeral art objects, so soon thrown into the waste-paper basket, images of our times, I regret the loss of them to future centuries which won't know us, or hardly. Vuitton the trunk dealer ... has sent an original card signed "Grignon": blue branches, green leaves, pink, red and white flowers rise from a rather small, faintly royal blue vase, a Gubbio shape, but modern....

I think I'd give first prize to Lalique – who started the trend. On an invitation to an exhibition of glassware, he conveyed the impression of sculptured glass to perfection, simply by embossing on plain white cards a chaste nest of leaves in which a pair of white pigeons are sitting in blissful solemnity.'

THE FIRST 'DESIGNER' PACKAGING

During the 1920s, particularly in Paris, there was a coincidence of art and advertising which produced the most elegant ephemera of all time. Modern art was new and exciting; at the same time, advertising was reaching unprecedented levels of sophistication. Letterheads, cards, packets, wrapping-paper – all were carefully considered and designed to impress the client with their prettiness and good taste. Gimpel, of course, was right – much was immediately committed to the waste-paper basket and lost. But, perhaps because he was not alone in his admiration, much has survived.

Lalique was a master and a pioneer in this field. The first artist to issue advertising cards, in 1919, he had designed a cardboard box for Coty's face-powder ten years earlier which continued to be used for more than half a century. The circular box is covered in a design of powder puffs in orange, black, gold and white – very much an Art Deco colour scheme. A decade later, sweets, gloves, writing-paper and much else was sold in stylish, colourful boxes. On some the design incorporated the manufacturer's or retailer's name, on some not.

Cadbury's commissioned designs for chocolate boxes from nine leading painters, including Laura Knight; the Italian confectionery company Sarotti had packaging designed for it by the German graphic artist Julius Gipkins. The artist Walter Kampmann designed wrapping-paper for the Elberfeld parfumier Morisse, and Yardley packed its 'April Violets' scent in paper designed by the British architect Reco Capey.

As well as ephemera designed by known artists there is much more that is unattributed. Quantities of bookmatches, matchbox labels, playing cards and stationery can be found emblazoned with Art Deco motifs.

There are Art Deco cigarette cards and cigarette boxes. Two of the latter are particularly famous: the Gitanes box featuring a gypsy dancer wreathed in curling smoke is still used today, while the Du Maurier box with its austere geometry in red, black and silver has become a collec-

**Pochoir print
by George Barbier**
16 x 15cm (print area)
Pruskin Gallery, London
Price: £25

**'Masked', etching and drypoint
by Louis Icart**
33 × 21.5cm
Sold: Sotheby's, New York, 19/6/86
Price: $935

tor's item. Even cigars were decorated; those by the Hamburg firm of L. Wolff were adorned with a very smart label designed by the Viennese artist C.O. Czeschka.

Paper fans, used for advertising, are an attractive form of Art Deco ephemera. Unfortunately, owing to their fragility, not many have survived. Like so many other elegant creations, they seem to have originated in Poiret's studios, and the Atelier Martine made many examples advertising the couturier's Rosine perfumes. Other fans included those designed by the cartoonist and interior designer Paul Iribe, for the Château de Madrid, a Paris restaurant. There were also fans advertising the leading Parisian department stores, seaside resorts such as La Baule – 'La plus belle plage d'Europe' – as well as a whole range of products and various services.

THE POCHOIR PROCESS

René Gimpel continued the diary entry quoted above as follows: 'I'll certainly be going to Cartier's; he's invited me to an exhibition of his modern jewellery designed by Barbier. It has been left to Barbier to get me there by sending one of his charming reproductions, a chic Parisian girl in a short, blue skirt patterned with large pink flowers.' George Barbier was one of the masters of the French Art Deco print, and the invitation card would have been produced by the 'pochoir' process. This technique of using stencils to make coloured prints was refined in France during the last quarter of the nineteenth century by printmakers who had been impressed by the stencils imported from Japan, where they were employed for printing cloth.

The pochoir process requires, in the first place, an analysis of the constituent colours in the original composition (usually a watercolour or gouache); then a stencil is cut for the areas of each different colour. The printer matches every pigment

Lithographic poster by Remigius Geyling
39.5 x 26cm
Sold: Sotheby's, London, 16/5/86
Price (including 2 other designs):
£110

and its density, and then applies the colour with squat brushes of short, soft bristle (*pompons*) over a black-and-white reproduction (often a collotype) of the original design. 'The advantages of the stencilling process', wrote the English painter Paul Nash in 1932, 'are obvious. The colour for each picture is applied separately by hand, not impressed by a mechanical device. The colours used are pure and permanent – the colours used in the originals – instead of being anything but pure and any distance you like from the originals. Furthermore, the drawings 77 admit of two qualities that no flat printing can give: texture and variety. In short, they are alive instead of being dead.'

Such an intricate technique, requiring the laborious employment of manual skill, is typical of French Art Deco. No effort was spared to produce objects which would satisy wealthy clients' demand for luxury and quality. Lacquerwork is one outstanding example; the art of pochoir is another. But whereas lacquered furniture by one of the Art Deco masters is, to all intents and purposes, unobtainable today, pochoir prints were produced in such quantities that examples are readily available at modest prices.

Pochoir print by E.G. Benito
37 x 27cm
Pruskin Gallery, London
Price: £140

FRENCH POCHOIR FASHION ILLUSTRATION

In 1908 Paul Poiret issued an album of his fashions printed by the pochoir process, with drawings commissioned from Paul Iribe. The illustrations of *Les Robes de Paul Poiret Racontées par Paul Iribe* were witty and brightly coloured, presenting a bold contrast to the sombre tertiary hues of Art Nouveau. Three years after the Fauves had first shocked spectators at the Salon with their uncouth palette, Parisians now accepted – expected, even – bright colours. So Poiret chose pochoir as a means of graphic reproduction. He published a second album in 1911, after Parisians had been further dazzled by the barbarous colours of Diaghilev's Ballets Russes. This time he employed a young painter, Georges Lepape, to design the illustrations for it.

Such was the success of Poiret's albums that Lucien Vogel, art director of the magazine *Femina*, took the opportunity to launch a periodical which would publish pochoir-printed illustrations of contemporary fashions. *La Gazette du Bon Ton* was published from 1912 to 1925, and among the artists whose work was reproduced in its pages were Georges Lepape, George Barbier, Edouard Garcia Benito, Robert Bonfils, Pierre Brissaud, Umberto Brunelleschi, Erté, Charles Martin, André Marty and José de Zamora. Other magazines featuring pochoir illustrations followed: *Journal des Dames et des Modes* (1912–14), *Les Feuillets d'Art* (1919–20), also published by Vogel, and *Art, Goût, Beauté* (1920–30). George Barbier contributed to all these, as well as illustrating albums celebrating the

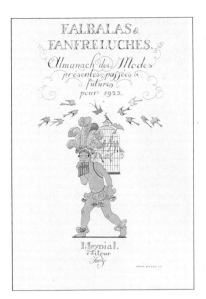

Title-page *Falbalas &*
Fanfreluches, **pochoir print by**
George Barbier
24.6 x 16cm
Pruskin Gallery, London
Price: £48

glass, metalwork, bookbindings etc., entitled *L'Art International d'Aujourd-'hui*, and there was another series called *Répertoire du Goût Moderne*. Some designers issued albums of pochoir illustrations which displayed their work, for instance Edouard Bénédictus, who produced three portfolios of designs for printed silks and satins, and Sonia Delaunay, whose *Compositions, Couleurs, Idées* appeared in 1930.

Single issues of the pochoir illustrated magazines or the almanacs, are rare. Complete runs are rarer still and impossibly expensive when they are offered for sale. But many copies of the magazines and albums have been broken up, and several of the illustrations were originally published loose anyway. Single pochoirs are comparatively inexpensive. Some were issued as individual pictures in large sizes suitable for framing; these are sometimes found in their original frames which often incorporate borders of tinted mirror glass.

Pochoir print
by Georges Lepape
29.2 x 28.5cm
Pruskin Gallery, London
Price: £300

genius of Nijinsky (1913) and Karsavina (1914), and producing a series of almanacs entitled *La Guirlande des Mois* from 1917 to 1921. This he followed with *Falbalas et Franfreluches*, a second series of almanacs published between 1922 and 1926, which, as well as Barbier's illustrations, carried writings by such darlings of *le haut monde* as Colette, the Comtesse Anna de Noailles and Cécile Sorel the actress.

The pochoir process was also used to illustrate books which described modern interior decoration. Charles Moreau published a series of volumes on contemporary sculpture,

**'Nonchalance', etching
by Max Brüning**

25 x 12cm

Sold: Phillips, London, 19/6/86

Price: £330

AMERICAN MAGAZINES

Most magazines of the 1920s and 1930s could not afford to have pochoir illustrations because they severely limited the number of copies that could be printed. Magazine advertising had become an important way of selling goods, particularly in America where there were no national newspapers, and advertisers preferred high-circulation journals. In Europe, because distribution was restricted by language barriers, publishers could not afford to pay the best artists, so it tended to be the American magazines that carried the finest Art Deco graphics. Four in particular attained high artistic standards: *Vogue, Harper's Bazaar, Vanity Fair* and *The New Yorker.* Their editors used the cream of European, as well as American, designers and illustrators.

Both *Vogue* and *Harper's Bazaar* went through two phases. During the first their graphic style was largely borrowed from Parisian magazines such as *Femina.* Erté, who worked in Poiret's studios before the First World War, was hired by *Harper's* to design its covers from 1915 to 1936. *Vogue* commissioned Georges Lepape to supply it with many of its covers, and both magazines frequently used Paris-based artists such as E.G. Benito, Charles Martin and André Marty. Two American artists who contributed drawings to *Vogue* very much in the Parisian style were George Wolf Plank and Helen Dryden.

The second phase began for *Vogue* in 1929 when the Russian-born graphic artist and photographer Mehemed Agha was appointed art director. He introduced more photography than was used previously, including work by Edward Steichen and Cecil Beaton, and he used sans-serif typefaces and other features of the Modernist graphic style which had been developed at the Bauhaus. Another Russian emigré, Alexey Brodovitch, who had worked in Paris before going to America in 1930, was appointed art director at *Harper's Bazaar* in 1934. There he introduced the same tendencies as Agha had done at *Vogue*. Among the artists who worked for the two magazines during this second phase were Herbert Matter, a Swiss designer who often incorporated photography in his graphics, and the notable French poster artist Cassandre, who designed covers for *Harper's Bazaar*.

Vanity Fair was perhaps the most sophisticated American magazine in the 1920s and 1930s, maintaining high standards of criticism, literary contributions and graphic design. Among those who contributed covers and illustrations were the French artists Jean Carlu, E.G. Benito, and Charles Martin, the Ukrainian Vladimir Bobritsky, the Italian Paolo Garretto and the Mexican Miguel Covarrubias, whose caricatures perfectly suited the magazine's witty style. Like *Vogue*, *Vanity Fair* was owned by Condé Nast, and many of the artists who contributed to it also had work published in *Vogue*.

Covarrubias also worked for *The New Yorker* to which Rose Silver and Ilonka Karasz, among others, contributed covers. Two other American publications which carried good Art Deco graphics were the business magazine *Fortune* and the small-circulation specialist periodical *Asia* which from 1924 had a series of fine Art Deco covers designed by Frank McIntosh.

EUROPEAN MAGAZINES

Some European magazines which regularly carried good Art Deco illustrations were: in France, *Femina*, *Le Rire* and *La Vie Parisienne*; in Germany, *Jugend*, *Die Woche* and *Die Dame*; in Italy, *La Rivista* and *Italia*; and in Spain, *Blanco y Negro*. Any copies of these are worth obtaining, because they nearly always included

Silhouette picture
22 x 19.5cm
Sold: Bonham's, London, 27/6/86
Price (including another similar):
£105

some interesting illustrations and usually had quite stylish covers.

Other magazines which occasionally contain Art Deco drawings, either as editorial or advertising illustrations, are the French *L'Illustration*, the English *Illustrated London News*, *The Sketch* and *The Graphic*, and the American *Woman's Home Companion* and *House Beautiful*. The 1920s and 1930s were the golden age of the illustrated magazine and the list of titles published is endless. Any discovered in second-hand bookshops are always worth looking through. Occasionally you will find a well-drawn, stylish illustration or advertisement.

81

Cover, *Harper's Bazaar*, by Erté
33.5 × 24.5cm
Pruskin Gallery, London
Price: £60

POSTERS

Referring to the early 1920s, Wolcott Gibbs wrote in *The New Yorker*: 'Advertising was the new giant loudspeaker of American free enterprise, the full-throated, blaring horn telling millions what to eat, what to drink, and what to wear.' Throughout the Western world it became impossible to avoid the advertisers' persistent hectoring. At one end of the scale were the elegant pochoir-printed cards discreetly dropped into Parisian letterboxes; at the other end were the stridently urged messages ending with happy jingles that began to seep over the American airwaves. In between there were the advertisements which appeared in newspapers and journals, and on posters, gaily decorating the urban landscape with colourful images of an exciting, glamorous world. By the 1920s the technology of lithographic printing had been fully developed, and posters went up all over Europe.

The relative condition of any poster significantly affects its value. Posters are printed in a large format on cheap paper, intended to last only a few weeks. Not many from the Art Deco period have survived undamaged. To quote from some introductory notes in the catalogue of a poster auction held by Phillips in New York a few years ago: 'Most important to the condition of a poster ... is the image of the poster: Is that image (the lines, the colour, the overall design) still clearly expressed? If so, it is a poster worth collecting.'

Many poster dealers use a simple system of rating condition. 'A' indicates that the colours are fresh and there is nothing missing; there may be a slight blemish or tear but this is at, or very near, the margin and not noticeable. Condition 'B' posters may have suffered a slight loss of paper, but not in any area crucial to the design; the colours are good although the paper may have yellowed. A poster rated as condition 'C' may

Souvenir brochure Chicago World's Fair 1933
22.8 × 30.6cm
Fred Marcus, M12 Antiquarius, London
Price: £12

have yellowed more severely, and folds or flaking may be quite visible, but otherwise the image is clear and the colour only a little faded. A good part of condition 'D' posters may be missing, including some of the design; colours are so faded and lines so obscure that it is impossible to appreciate the artist's original intention. The condition rating obviously affects the price, but by a variable factor depending on the importance of the artist and the rarity of the design. Condition 'D' posters are really not worth buying, and it is wise to look out for restorations when offered examples in condition 'A'.

Art Deco poster artists were legion – far too many to list. The work of only a handful is prohibitively expensive, a group which includes A.M. Cassandre (as Adolphe Mouron signed himself), Jean Dupas, Charles Loupot, René Vincent, Paul Colin, Edward McKnight-Kauffer and Joseph Binder. But it is particular images rather than artists' reputations which tend to determine the value of a poster. A famous example of this is the highly prized poster for Daudé pianos, which combines three important features characteristic of the Art Deco posters: the overhead view, the composition tilted towards the diagonal, and strong colours. It was designed by François Daudé, the owner of the piano company, who never did any other posters.

A recurring image in Art Deco posters is of a steamship's bows soaring into the sky. Cassandre originated it in a poster advertising the liner *L'Atlantique*; the same idea was used by W.F. Ten Broek in a poster for the Holland-America steamship line, and another variation on the theme was the poster for the Cunard Line, designed in the studio of Alexey Brodovitch. Another motif which contains the essence of Art Deco is the motor-car, preferably depicted travelling at speed. The classic example is a poster designed by Charles Loupot for Phillippossian Automobiles, where the speeding roadster, surrounded by swirling clouds of dust and smoke, is driven by a girl whose flaming red hair streams behind her in the airflow.

Three subjects were treated by several different artists who attained consistently high standards of design when working on them. The subjects were PKZ, a Swiss menswear company; Mistinguett, the Parisian cabaret artiste; and the London Underground Railway. Between them these three clients used some of the best Art Deco poster designers. During the 1920s PKZ employed several brilliant Swiss artists including Herbert Matter, Otto Morach, Otto Baumberger, Alex W. Diggelman, Karl Bickel and Hugo Laubi. Frank Pick, who ran the London Under-

**Handcoloured woodcut
by Reni Schaschl**
30.2 × 20.9cm
Pruskin Gallery, London
Price: £240

ground Railway during the 1920s, commissioned posters from several leading British artists including Frank Brangwyn, Aubrey Hammond, George Sheringham, Rex Whistler and Ashley Havinden, as well as the American Edward McKnight-Kauffer and the Frenchman Jean Dupas. Charles Gesmar designed posters for Mistinguett until his early death in 1928; then a number of artists took up the challenge, including Zig, G.K. Benda, Orsi, Rougemont and Jean-Dominique van Caulaert. Posters of the glamorous entertainer were issued as late as 1941, by which time the challenge must have been awesome – she was then aged sixty-six!

PAINTINGS AND DRAWINGS

Paintings, drawings and even prints by leading artists associated with Art Deco tend to be very expensive. Work by the recognized masters of the Ecole de Paris, in particular, always fetches high prices.

An artist whose prints brilliantly depicted the chic young woman of the 1930s was Louis Icart. He made colour etchings with aquatint of several hundred subjects. They were so enormously popular in the USA when they were first published that a Louis Icart society was formed to supervise their distribution.

Quite frequently the buyer may come across a painting or drawing signed with an illegible or unknown name, or not signed at all, which,

while no great work of art, neverthe-less perfectly captures the spirit of the Art Deco era. It might be just a portrait painted by an amateur of his or her favourite aunt. But, if the lady is wearing a cloche hat and perhaps smoking a cigarette through a long holder, and even – maybe – is sitting at the wheel of a Bugatti roadster, then it is a good Art Deco painting, even if the perspective of the wind-screen is incorrect.

Object	Quality of manufacture	Quality of design and/or decoration	Rarity	Price (£)	Price ($)
Anon.					
pochoir print	8	7	■	20-50	40-80
magazine cover	5	7	■	40-80	60-130
printed fan	4	6	■ ■ ■	60-120	100-200
lithographic poster	6	7	■	200-600	320-1000
Barbier, George					
pochoir print (theatre design)	8	9	■	40-80	60-130
pochoir print (fashion plate)	8	9	■	75-150	120-240
pochoir print (illustration)	8	9	■	100-300	160-480
Baumberger, Otto					
lithographic poster	6	9	■ ■	250-500	400-800
Benda, G.K.					
lithographic poster	6	8	■ ■ ■	200-400	320-640
Bénédictus, Edouard					
pochoir print (textile design)	8	8	■	50-100	80-160
Benito, Edouard-Garcia					
pochoir print	8	8	■ ■	40-100	60-160
Vogue cover	5	8	■ ■	50-150	80-240
Bobritsky, Vladimir					
magazine cover	5	8	■ ■ ■	50-100	80-160
Bonfils, Robert					
pochoir print	8	9	■ ■	50-100	80-160
lithographic poster (1925 Paris Exhibition)	6	9	■ ■ ■	900-1000+	1440-1600+
Brissaud, Pierre					
pochoir print	8	7	■ ■	40-80	60-130

Qualities on a scale 1-10   ■ Rare   ■ ■ Very rare   ■ ■ ■ Extremely rare

Object	Quality of manufacture	Quality of design and/or decoration	Rarity	Price (£)	Price ($)
Brunelleschi, Umberto					
pochoir print	8	8	■ ■	50-100	80-160
lithographic poster	6	8	■ ■ ■	500-750	800-1200
Carlu, Jean					
magazine cover	5	9	■ ■ ■	100-200	160-320
Cassandre (A. Mouron)					
Harper's Bazaar cover	5	10	■ ■ ■	150-300	240-480
Covarrubias, Miguel					
magazine cover	5	9	■ ■ ■	60-120	100-200
Delaunay, Sonia					
pochoir print (decorative design)	8	9	■ ■ ■	100-200	160-320
Diggelman, Alex					
lithographic poster	6	9	■ ■ ■	250-750	400-1200
Domergue, Jean-Gabriel					
lithographic poster	6	8	■ ■	300-600	480-1000
Drian, Etienne					
etching	8	8	■ ■	250-500	400-800
Dryden, Helen					
Vogue cover	5	8	■ ■ ■	60-120	100-200
Erté					
Harper's Bazaar cover	5	9	■ ■	150-250	240-400
pochoir print	9	9	■ ■	300-600	480-1000
watercolour/gouache	9	9	■ ■	400-1000+	640-1600+
Garretto, Paolo					
magazine cover	5	8	■ ■ ■	50-100	80-160

Qualities on a scale 1-10   ■ Rare   ■ ■ Very rare   ■ ■ ■ Extremely rare

Object	Quality of manufacture	Quality of design and/or decoration	Rarity	Price (£)	Price ($)
Gesmar, Charles					
lithographic poster	6	9	■ ■	200-500	320-800
Geyling, Remigius					
lithographic poster	6	8	■ ■ ■	100-200	160-320
Girbal, Anton					
lithographic poster	6	7	■ ■	200-500	320-800
Icart, Louis					
charcoal drawing	8	5	■ ■	200-400	320-640
etching and aquatint	8	7	■	300-1000+	480-1600+
Kiffer, Charles					
lithographic poster	6	7	■ ■	300-500	480-800
Laubi, Hugo					
lithographic poster	6	8	■ ■	600-1000	1000-1600
Lepape, Georges					
pochoir print (fashion plate)	8	9	■	50-150	80-240
pochoir print (illustration)	8	9	■	200-500	320-800
Vogue cover	5	9	■ ■	60-120	100-200
Martin, Charles					
pochoir print	8	7	■ ■	40-80	60-130
magazine cover	5	7	■ ■	40-80	60-130
Marty, André					
magazine cover	5	9	■ ■	60-120	100-200
pochoir print	8	9	■ ■	75-150	120-240
Ten Broek, W.F.					
lithographic poster	6	9	■ ■ ■	750-1000+	1200-1600+

Qualities on a scale 1-10   ■ Rare   ■ ■ Very rare   ■ ■ ■ Extremely rare

Object	Quality of manufacture	Quality of design and/or decoration	Rarity	Price (£)	Price ($)
Vertès, Marcel drawing, crayon/ink	8	7	■ ■ ■	200-400	320-640
Zamorra, José de pochoir print	8	8	■ ■	50-100	80-160
Zig lithographic poster	6	8	■ ■	300-600	480-1000

Qualities on a scale 1-10   ■ Rare   ■ ■ Very rare   ■ ■ ■ Extremely rare

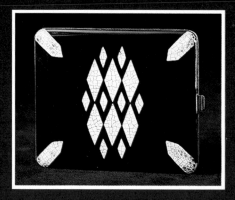

CHAPTER FIVE

METALWORK
AND
JEWELLERY

Enamelled cigarette case with
eggshell decoration. Galia Antiques,
Q4/5 Antiquarius, London. Price: £395.

The technological advances of the nineteenth century widened the scope of metalwork greatly. New methods of treating metals and new alloys were developed, as well as mechanical processes which led directly to the mass production of decorative metalwork. By the end of the century there were two distinct categories: mass-manufactured objects, and those which were handmade, the value of the latter often lying in the fact that they were built by craftsmen and not necessarily because they were made of more precious materials. At the time of the 1925 Exhibition in Paris, most of the exhibits were handmade and the fact that the mass-produced object was poorly represented indicates that in the mid-twenties it was still regarded with some contempt, although in Germany and Holland serious efforts were being made to assert its viability.

FRENCH METALWORK

In the early twenties the best metalwork was handmade, or at least hand-finished. Craftsman-designers were producing pieces which were copied in cheaper materials by imitators, but handmade objects were clearly still providing source material. The metalwork produced by Edgar Brandt was particularly influential but it is prohibitively expensive. Only slightly more accessible is metalwork made by the French craftsmen Raymond Subes, Paul Kiss and Gilbert Poillerat who imitated Brandt's style. Their work is often decorated with formalized, natural shapes – such as animals, flowers, birds and so on. In turn, they in-

Hammered brass and iron firescreen
Height: 91 cm
Sold: Sotheby's, New York, 19/6/86
Price: $1320

fluenced the design of radiator grilles, decorative gates and other pieces which were mass-produced in less expensive materials for new apartment blocks and houses on the Continent and in America.

In the twenties, Jean Dunand was making vases which were hammered from sheet copper, steel, pewter or silver, and then enriched with inlays of different alloys or metals, or with lacquer. He experimented with the natural process of oxidization to produce metallic blacks, and with materials such as steel, zinc and aluminium which he used for their various finishes. His vases were simple in their overall shape, to give maximum emphasis to the rich surfaces which sometimes bear more resemblance to costly and exotic fabrics than to metal.

Gabriel Lacroix used pewter, zinc, silver, gold and platinum to create relief sculptures, which were constructed from thin sheets of metal moulded over wooden forms. He exploited combinations of metals to produce contrasts and to give the finished reliefs depth and clarity. His own work, and that of the pupils he taught at the Ecole des Arts Appliqués, was carefully finished; the joining point of each sheet with another was very carefully concealed and particular attention was given to the contrast of polished and textured surfaces.

Lacroix's work had considerable influence in the area of mass-produced decorative arts; it is possible to find metal-relief decorations on all sorts of objects from the late twenties – on cigarette boxes, for example, or even on fenders made to go around fireplaces. (In the late thirties a series of cigarette cards was produced by W.D. and H.O. Wills in

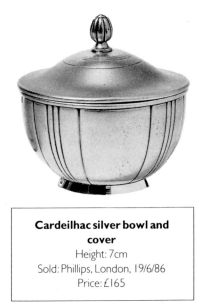

Cardeilhac silver bowl and cover
Height: 7cm
Sold: Phillips, London, 19/6/86
Price: £165

metal-relief; with the album came a sheet of hints on the decorative potential of the cards when applied to furniture, boxes etc.) Metal-relief was still an important element of interior design in the thirties. In America it can be seen, among other places, on the exterior and interior surfaces of the Rockefeller Centre, and in England in the richly decorated foyer of the Daily Express Building designed in 1936 by Sir Owen Williams.

Copper was often used by French metalworkers in the early twenties. Claudius Linossier, who was Dunand's pupil, produced vases and bowls in copper which were deliberately primitive in appearance and often irregular in their outlines. Unlike his master he chose not to patinate or lacquer the base material but to use it for its particular colour and to rely on texture rather than colour contrast for effect. Other cop-

Enamelled cigarette case
8 x 9.5cm
Galia Antiques, Q4/5 Antiquarius,
London
Price: £35

which are abstractions from natural forms in sweet colours: pastel blues, pinks and greens. These have been extensively faked recently, particularly examples with the more geometric style of decoration.

Silver tea and coffee services were being mass produced in the twenties but the style of the pieces made for the general market tended to be relentlessly traditional and manufactured by power pressing silver on to a

Austrian enamelled cigarette case
8.5 x 4.5cm
Sold: Phillips, London, 19/6/86
Price: £187

persmiths of the period include Berthe Cazin, Gaston Bigard, Jean Serrière and Luclanel who worked for the firm Orfèvrerie Christofle.

Apart from the tea and coffee services produced by this company in the twenties, it made a number of hand-crafted vases with basic shapes and surface designs taken from 'primitive' art. One example is obviously influenced in its shape and colouring by Inca pottery vessels; the designs were translated into silver and turquoise enamel with a regular pattern of diamond shaped motifs on both surfaces of the vase.

Enamelling, which had been popular at the turn of the century in Art Nouveau metalwork, was still used in the twenties. The sculptor Gustave Miklos made enamelled plaques with abstract designs, but these are extremely rare. More accessible are the vases produced by Camille Fauré, who worked in Limoges and produced a series of vases enamelled on to various base metals in designs

steel matrix. The silverware which is most obviously Art Deco was handmade, sometimes by independent designers and sometimes by craftsmen working for established companies. Christofle, for instance, commissioned designs from Paul Follot, Süe et Mare and the Danish designer Christian Fjerdingstad, which were based on clean, geometric shapes with little or no surface decoration.

Jean Puiforcat made tea and coffee services in silver which are at the same time functional and extremely luxurious. The pieces he exhibited in

1925 were beaten silver, but he also produced sets in polished silver with simple cylindrical or rectangular forms offset by knobs and handles of ivory, jade, lapis lazuli and hardwood. Such apparent simplicity demands a very high standard of craftsmanship and minute attention to detail. All of Puiforcat's work – the sets, individual pieces and the clocks he made in silver in the thirties – show the same refinement and excellence of workmanship. Puiforcat's designs have continued with few modifications into the 1980s.

FRENCH JEWELLERY AND ACCESSORIES

The designs which appear in de luxe jewellery in France, most particularly in pieces produced for the *grandes maisons* of Paris – Boucheron, Cartier, Van Cleef and Arpels and Lacloche Frères – exerted a considerable influence on the mass market. Where the buying public might be hesitant about new and fashionable design in their homes, they were happy to accept it in items of personal decoration. In Europe and America, costumes and jewellery which have the stylistic elements we usually associate with Art Deco were being worn even before the style was established in interior design or architecture.

De luxe jewellery of the twenties was influenced in its design by Oriental art, by the exotic designs of Léon Bakst for the Ballets Russes, by African art and by Cubism. The *grandes maisons* were producing pieces made in precious metals with precious and semi-precious stones. Coral and jade were particularly favoured because of their colours and because they could be carved. Frosted crystal,

which had been used before the war by Lalique, was still important and often used in conjunction with black enamel or onyx.

The straight silhouette of twenties fashion demanded new forms of jewellery; earrings, for example, were elongated as women wore their hair shorter. One particularly typical design which was used by all the houses was the pendant earring consisting of a series of links, often encrusted with tiny diamonds, and terminating in a drop of carved jade, coral or crystal. Necklaces too were longer, with the main decorative emphasis falling at chest rather than throat level. The pendant was a favoured form for the new necklaces; some are almost tiny pieces of sculpture which hang from decorated chains or else from silk cords which are threaded at intervals with carved beads in the Chinese manner.

Christofle silver-plated ice bucket and tongs
Height: 16.8cm
Galia Antiques, Q4/5 Antiquarius, London
Price: £220

In the twenties the same design influences as existed elsewhere were to be found in fashion accessories. The cigarette cases, powder compacts and vanity cases that the jewellery houses made for the fashionable woman were often markedly Oriental, Egyptian or African in their decoration. Cartier manufactured a range of cigarette cases decorated with tiny jewelled plaques depicting formalized birds or flowers and set against a background of Chinese yellow enamel. Boucheron used carved coral and brilliants to create a single motif against a black ground, and several companies made variations on the theme of the Oriental seal as a motif. Egyptianesque patterns, usually in enamels of various colours, were much favoured, but it seems to be the African-influenced pieces which produced the most innovative and exciting designs; Paul Brandt, for example, used crackled eggshell lacquer contrasted with enamel in brilliant red or dense black to make stylized African designs.

The work of the *grandes maisons*, and of designers like Gérard Sandoz, Henri Miault and René Robert was both exclusive and very expensive, but it was widely imitated and designs which obviously derive from their work were mass produced at every level. In inexpensive costume jewellery the new plastics were used to simulate coral and jade, and various metal alloys replaced the silver, gold and platinum of the originals. Transfer printing was used on cigarette cases, compacts and vanity cases made for the mass market and some of these were sold very cheaply through chain stores such as Woolworth. As the decade advanced costume jewellery achieved a new status. Coco Chanel is generally credited with having made 'fakes' respectable and certainly by the end of the twenties pieces which are very obviously not 'the real thing' were selling in department stores and fashion shops. Huge pearls were a particular favourite, especially in pink or grey, and plastic bangles were produced which were worn in quantities in the manner of Nancy Cunard.

Silver tea set, Sheffield 1935
Height (hot water jug): 20cm
Sold: Sotheby's, London, 16/5/86
Price: £495

In the thirties the de luxe designs of the previous decade were simply no longer appropriate either to the new fashions in clothing or to the mood of French society. The Colonial Exhibition held in Paris in 1931 introduced a new repertoire of ethnic forms to French designers, who responded by producing pieces which were deliberately 'barbaric' in their appearance, and often made from the wide variety of plastics available by that time. Fornell made brooches in stylized animal shapes and bangles moulded in dramatic forms. The Printemps department store in Paris sold cuff bracelets in silvered or gilded metal or carved from horn. The *grandes maisons* responded to the fashion for African design by producing ranges of dramatic jewellery in coloured enamels; Mauboussin made necklaces of metal flowers enriched with small brilliants; Cartier produced a range of 'Blackamoor' clips and earrings, a negro head with a jewelled turban and collar. While hardly African, these designs can be seen as part of the passion for the exotic, and they caught the public imagination sufficiently to be reproduced *ad nauseam* in gilt and enamel.

By far the most influential designs made by the de luxe houses were the versatile clips sometimes called 'cocktail clips' made originally in platinum and diamonds. These could be worn as one brooch or separated into two pieces and clipped to a hat, a bag or a belt. Clips were mass produced throughout the thirties, and marcasite on silver replaced the platinum and diamonds in some good, popularly priced pieces. French paste on silver was another alternative; Woolworth marketed a range of *diamanté* and nickel clips which certainly had all the glitter of

Silver-plated coffee cups and saucers designed by Louis Süe
Height (cup): 7cm
Sold: Sotheby's, London, 16/5/86
Price (set of 6): £209

the real thing even if the stones had a tendency to fall out almost at once.

A few, individual designers drew inspiration from the machine aesthetic for their jewellery. Jean Fouquet, for example, made a bracelet in 1932, of ebonite rings enclosing chromed ball bearings which were held in place by screws, the heads of which were left exposed. These designs, however, had little influence on the mass market. They were costly because they were regarded as 'designs'; the purchaser was paying for the concept not the materials.

GERMAN METALWORK

The French influence in metalwork and jewellery was felt across Europe and America in the decades between the Wars. Its prominence in these areas still persisted when its direct influence in furniture design and ar-

97

chitecture was diminishing. Even so, other countries were producing metalwork of a high standard and a marked individuality. In Germany, the metal workshop at the Weimar Bauhaus was designing and making silverware which combined absolute simplicity of form with a high standard of craftsmanship. Tea services by Christian Dell, for example, were made from polished silver with dark hardwood handles and knobs with clean, dramatic sculptural shapes.

After the Bauhaus moved to Dessau in 1925 the emphasis of the metal workshop turned from the production of craftsman-built pieces to metalwork that could be mass produced. The forms used by designers such as Marianne Brandt and Wilhelm Wagenfeld were based on the basic geometric shapes of the cylinder, the sphere and the hemisphere, and because cost was an important consideration, cheaper materials such as brass and nickelsilver replaced solid silver.

It is probably in the field of lighting and interior fittings that the Bauhaus had its widest influence, and certainly its greatest commercial success. Marianne Brandt, Hans Przyrembel and Karl Jucker designed and made lamps and lights which were radical in their simplicity and in their suitability for the modern interior. The adjustable ceiling light designed by Brandt and Przyrembel is a perfect example of this, with its hemispherical shade and chromed rods and cylinders. It was designed to be pulled down to give an intense and local light, or pushed up to give a more diffused lighting to a whole room. This and other light fittings and lamps were industrially produced by Schwintzer & Graff, and Körting & Matthiessen (who mar-

keted them as the 'Kandem' range).

The influence of Bauhaus metalwork was widespread. It is particularly evident in the work of Jean Perzel, a lighting specialist who designed for a number of private clients and who was commissioned to produce the lights for the liner *Normandie*. In America, Donald Deskey and Eugene Schoen adapted Bauhaus forms and materials for lighting in the Rockefeller Centre, and in England the same spherical and cylindrical shapes appear in the electric fan heaters designed by Christian Barman for HMV in 1934.

Often the Bauhaus influence was translated into a wilful freakishness, probably because the geometric simplicity of Brandt and Przyrembel's designs were seen as 'geometry for geometry's sake', and real attention to function was ignored. An electroplated coffee set designed for the Monza exhibition in Italy by a British

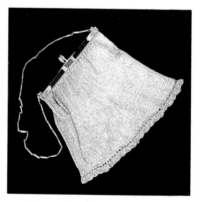

Silver mesh purse
Width: 11cm
Galia Antiques, Q4/5 Antiquarius,
London
Price: £120

firm in 1930 is a perfect example of this: the teapot, and cream and hot water jugs are composed of a series of trapezoid shapes with sharply angled handles designed, it seems, to give acute pain to the user.

METALWORK IN SCANDINAVIA

In Denmark the Georg Jensen workshop was producing silverware and jewellery which was known and admired in France in the twenties. Jensen and his chief designer Johan Rohde used a style which is quite distinct from that which evolved in France and Germany, since it was based on natural form and decorated with ornaments borrowed directly from nature. It is, however, most emphatically not Art Nouveau. The curving lines are tightly disciplined and the flower, fruit and animal forms which appear on Jensen's tea services, bowls and candlesticks, are arranged in formal clusters rather than in linear curves. The cutlery designed for Jensen by Rohde in 1915 and the five-branched candlesticks of 1921 were particularly admired in Paris. Kay Bojesen, who trained in Jensen's workshop before setting up as an independent designer, made silver pieces which bear some resemblance to those made by Puiforcat; he used simple shapes with no surface decoration and is best known for his extremely elegant table silver.

> **Paste, silver and cabochon onyx bracelet**
> Length: 18cm
> Galia Antiques, Q4/5 Antiquarius, London
> Price: £395

In Norway, the David Andersen company of Oslo employed a team of young artists to design metalware for mass production; the simple stylishness and sculptural quality of their pieces recur in the metalwork produced in Scandinavia in the 1950s.

AMERICAN METALWORK AND JEWELLERY

In the USA metalwork from the period between the Wars tends to fall into two clear categories: one which followed the Arts and Crafts tradition begun in England in the nineteenth century; and one which adapted the ideas of European Modernism to American taste. There is, however, also a third category which has nothing to do with either Modernism or Arts and Crafts and which is primarily to do with jewellery design.

The largest of the Arts and Crafts groups called itself 'The Roycrofters' and marketed its work through the Roycroft Copper Shop and the Roycroft catalogues. It was a large team of craftsmen, headed by Karl Kipp and Dard Hunter, who produced a

relationship of forms and attention to texture in many of the pieces.

Modernism came to America in the late twenties and its impact can be seen first in the work of the established designers. The metalwork produced by Raymond Hood, the architect of the Chicago Tribune Building, shows a clear influence of 'machine styling' – the table lamps and standard lamps in his room for the 1929 Metropolitan Museum of Modern Art exhibition are composed of chromed rectangular rods rising in trio from a conical base. Outside New York, Eliel Saarinen was designing metalwork at the Cranbrook Academy, which used the same hemispherical and vertical elements as Brandt's designs for the Bauhaus. Mass-produced metalwork inspired by such pieces were on sale in the late twenties at shops like Macy's and Lord & Taylor.

In the early thirties the designer Russel Wright was experimenting with spun aluminium, making tea services and table accessories with emphatically spherical forms. These were subsequently mass produced and sold through department stores and Wright's own showrooms in New York. In 1933 he made the prototypes

wide range of household objects in copper and wrought iron. From the early part of the century their work was characterized by simplicity of form, stylized decoration derived from plants, trees and so on, and a very obviously 'hand-worked' finish. In the twenties Roycroft work shows some Art Deco influence while still retaining an obviously 'crafted' look.

The metalworkers based in and around Chicago were also influenced by Arts and Crafts, but in their case the influence came via Frank Lloyd Wright – whose designs by the turn of the century were already based on geometric forms. The Kalo shops opened in Chicago by Clara Barck Welles were an outlet for handcrafted but very stylish silverware in the twenties. Kalo silver has none of the 'folksy' quality of Roycroft metal work and the influence of Lloyd Wright is often evident in the careful

**Silver and rosewood vase
by Jean Puiforcat**
Height: 10.5cm
Sold: Phillips, London, 19/6/86
Price: £330

for a range of silver flatware in absolutely geometric shapes and in 1935, as consultant designer to the Chase Brass Company, he devised a range of domestic utensils which were to be made in chromed brass. His work was successful enough to be imitated; the ALCOA company brought out a line of aluminium pieces in 1931 which are very obviously inspired by Wright.

Metal, along with plastic and glass, was the material most favoured by the new industrial designers of the thirties. Henry Dreyfuss, Norman Bel Geddes, Raymond Loewy and Walter Dorwin Teague all designed for large companies in the States. Items like Dreyfuss's toaster for the Birtman Electric Co., designed in mirror chrome and black Bakelite, are splendid pieces of industrial Art Deco.

Jewellery design in America was heavily influenced by Paris; the large and fashionable stores in the big cities sold designer pieces imported from France, and Cartier had a shop of its own in New York. In Hollywood Paul Flato was producing jewellery which had a particularly American glamour; while it was influenced by the work of Cartier and Boucheron it was rather more exuberant. One of his most widely imitated pieces was a shooting star trailing behind it an arc of smaller stars made from tiny brilliants. Flato's work, along with Cartier's, was used in the films of the thirties and seen (and desired) by huge numbers of people. His influence on the mass market was therefore considerable.

ENGLISH METALWORK AND JEWELLERY

In England, as in America, the Arts and Crafts movement had a lasting effect on metalwork. It was this, along with a marked conservatism in design, which gave rise to the criticism levelled at the British pavilion in the 1925 Paris Exhibition. There were exceptions however. Individual craftsmen were producing designs in

Silver bowl by Charles Boyton
Diameter: 12.5cm
Sold: Phillips, London, 21/10/86
Price: £209

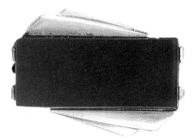

keeping with the modern movement, and companies were making pieces which were sometimes both exciting and radical in their forms. For example, the Napper and Davenport Company of Birmingham produced the 'Cube' teapot in 1922. Made from silver with a wooden handle and knob, the teapot incorporates both the handle and the spout within its overall cube shape. The design is both practical and extremely stylish.

The Bauhaus ideals of clarity of form, practicality and mass production were very well understood by the English designer Harold Stabler. At the same time his work is very stylish. In the tea set he designed for Adie Bros of Birmingham the teapot, water jug, creamer and sugar basin are arranged to form a compact square on the tray that accommodates them, which is also rectangular; the cube is broken only by the handles of the teapot and water jug and those of the tray. Stabler used hardwood for the knob on the teapot and ivory for the jug to distinguish

the two pieces, which are otherwise identical. Adie Bros manufactured the set in silver in 1935 and then in electroplate a year later. The less expensive version reached a wide market and was one of Adie's best-selling designs. Other English crafts-man-designers included Edward Spencer, Bernard Cuzner, Charles Boyton and Robert Goodden, who were all producing pieces which reflected Continental Art Deco.

Walter Patrick Belk, designing for Roberts & Belk of Sheffield, produced some simple but elegant designs for cutlery which are quite different from the reproduction styles favoured by Sheffield in the twenties. His designs in electroplate were used in the dining rooms of the liner *Queen Mary* and proved to be so popular that they were later used in the *Queen Elizabeth*.

In 1929 an American photographer, Curtis Moffat, opened his gallery at 4 Fitzroy Square in London with the intention of selling examples of avant-garde design as well as luxury items like jewellery and porcelain. Among his regular stock were pieces of metalwork by Desny, who made stylish cocktail shakers from silver or chrome plate with phenolic handles and dramatic bowls with fin-like supports, again in silver. Desny's range included silver beakers and jugs intended for use and display as cocktail equipment. His work was extensively copied by mass manufacturers in cheaper materials and influenced the design of other modern domestic accessories.

Curtis Moffat occasionally worked with Duncan Miller, and his influence is evident in Miller's exhibit at the Dorland Hall Exhibition of 1933 where metals were used for standard lamps in conjunction with opaque glass bowl shades. Moffat was particularly interested in the use of metals in the modern interior, and although his shop closed down in 1932 he had brought decorative metalwork to the attention of fashionable London at least. He was certainly not single-handedly responsible for the acceptance of Modernist metalwork in this country, but by appealing to high fashion he bypassed the preconceived ideas that metal was 'cold', 'clinical' and 'utilitarian'. In the thirties an increasing amount of chromed steel was being used in the manufacture of light fittings, ash trays, plant holders and magazine racks, by companies like Cox & Co. and PEL.

Asprey of Bond Street marketed pieces of French de luxe jewellery throughout the period and produced their own designs which show a marked French influence. One of their best-selling items was the vanity case originally designed by Cartier which incorporated a powder compact, lipstick holder, cigarette case and purse in one rectangular box. These were copied for the mass market, made in chrome-plated metal for the chain stores and in silver plate for wealthier clients.

New York World's Fair 1939 brass ashtray
Diameter: 11.5cm
Fred Marcus, M12 Antiquarius,
London
Price: £15

Object	Quality of manufacture	Quality of design and/or decoration	Rarity	Price (£)	Price ($)
Bracelets, bangles					
carved ivory bangle, (upper arm)	7	7	■ ■	40-200	60-320
metal cuff bracelet	7	8	■ ■ ■	50-150	80-240
moulded catalin bangle, made for Printemps	7	8	■ ■	50-70	80-110
plastic bangle	7	7	■ ■	25-60	45-100
wide bracelet, paste on silver in a geometric pattern	7	8	■ ■	50-150	80-240
Brooches					
carved glass buckle with paste on a metal back	6	7	■ ■	25-35	45-55
carved glass in gold mount	7	8	■ ■	100-150	160-240
circular, onyx, jade and brilliants, style of Boucheron	8	8	■ ■	700-1000	1120-1600
Egyptian-style, plastics with scarab	6	7	■ ■ ■	40-60	60-100
Modernist, chrome, onyx and coral	7	7	■ ■	150-250	240-400
Modernist, chrome and plastic	6	7	■	25-50	45-80
Cigarette cases					
enamel/eggshell lacquer on silver	9	8	■ ■ ■	600-900	1000-1440
enamel on gold, Cartier	9	8	■ ■	900-1000+	1440-1600+
engraved silver, Asprey	8	7	■ ■	250-300	400-480
transfer-printed on to metal	5	6	■	5-25	10-45
Cigarette holders					
long holder in coloured casein with gold bands	7	7	■ ■	15-40	30-60
silver with ambroid mouthpiece in silver case	7	6	■	15-30	30-50
Clocks					
chrome geometric clock, black face with chrome digits	7	7	■ ■ ■	15-40	30-50

Qualities on a scale 1-10   ■ Rare   ■ ■ Very rare   ■ ■ ■ Extremely rare

Object	Quality of manufacture	Quality of design and/or decoration	Rarity	Price (£)	Price ($)
Clocks, contd					
silver travelling clock, enamel face,	8	7	■ ■	250-500	400-800
Cocktail equipment					
chrome shaker	7	7	■	15-30	30-50
cocktail set, Desny for Curtis Moffat	7	8	■ ■ ■	300-500	480-800
silver shaker, Mappin & Webb	8	7	■ ■	150-250	240-400
silver plate shaker	7	7	■	60-80	100-130
Compacts					
enamel on gold, Cartier	9	8	■ ■	800-1000+	1280-1600+
enamel, translucent, over engine-turned silver	8	6	■ ■	100-250	160-400
Decorative metalwork					
metal radiator cover, style of Brandt	7	6	■ ■	250-500	400-800
pair of glass doors with chromed metal	7	7	■ ■	400-600	640-1000
pair of glass doors dec. ironwork	7	7	■ ■ ■	800-1000	1280-1600
pair of wrought iron gates	8	7	■ ■	600-900	1000-1440
Earrings					
black plastic clips with paste	6	7	■	10-25	20-45
carved jade pendant, gold chains	7	8	■ ■	60-200	100-320
diamanté on nickel clips	5	6	■	10-15	20-30
diamonds on platinum clips, Cartier	9	6	■ ■	900-1000+	1440-1600+
etched or carved glass pendant on gold chains	7	8	■ ■	40-200	60-320
marcasite drops with coral or onyx pendant	7	8	■ ■	40-80	60-130
pair of clips, paste on silver, geometric pattern	7	7	■	35-60	55-100
pair of marcasite and onyx clips joining to make a brooch	7	7	■	50-75	80-120

Qualities on a scale 1-10   ■ Rare   ■ ■ Very rare   ■ ■ ■ Extremely rare   **105**

Object	Quality of manufacture	Quality of design and/or decoration	Rarity	Price (£)	Price ($)
Evening bags, necessaires					
enamelled necessaire on silver	8	8	■ ■	400-700	640-1120
silver mesh evening purse on silver frame with chain handle	7	6	■ ■	30-80	50-130
silver necessaire with cabochon clasp, Cartier	8	8	■ ■	800-1000+	1280-1600+
transfer-printed metal necessaire, cord strap	6	6	■ ■	15-40	30-60
Lamps					
chrome standard lamp, opaque glass shade	6	6	■ ■	150-200	240-320
chrome table lamp, opaque glass shade	6	6	■ ■	80-120	130-200
pair of bronze mask wall lights	7	8	■ ■	320-500	510-800
pair of chrome and frosted glass fan-shaped wall lights	6	7	■ ■	40-80	60-130
pair of chrome and frosted glass shell-shaped wall lights	6	7	■ ■	40-80	60-130
Necklaces					
beads in imitation of carved coral	6	6	■ ■	10-15	20-30
carved coral pendant on gold chain with coral beads	8	8	■ ■	400-600	640-1000
carved glass pendant with small brilliants, gold mount	8	8	■ ■ ■	350-500	560-800
coloured wooden beads with small gold coloured beads between	6	7	■ ■	25-30	45-50
engraved ivory pendant on silk cord with silk tassel	8	8	■ ■ ■	400-600	640-1000
Modernist pendant, chrome, jade, onyx and coral	7	8	■	150-300	240-480
Modernist pendant, nickel and plastics on geom. link nickel chain	6	7	■ ■	25-50	45-80
moulded celluloid pendant with flower design, hand-tinted on silk cord with beads and tassel	7	8	■	100-150	160-240

Qualities on a scale 1-10   ■ Rare   ■ ■ Very rare   ■ ■ ■ Extremely rare

Object	Quality of manufacture	Quality of design and/or decoration	Rarity	Price (£)	Price ($)
Necklaces contd					
paste on silver in a geom. pattern	7	8	■ ■	100-200	160-320
plastic pendant in Egyptian style, with scarab on silk cord with beads	7	8	■ ■ ■	100-150	160-240
Rings					
gold ring, large opal with stepped diamond shoulders	7	8	■ ■	900-1000+	1440-1600+
marcasite on silver ring	6	7	■	25-50	45-80
paste and chrysoberyl ring on silver	7	7	■ ■	80-150	130-240
paste and onyx on silver, set in a geometric pattern	7	8	■ ■	100-150	160-240
plastic ring made in imitation of jade, ivory or coral	6	7	■	15-30	30-50
Table lighters					
chrome airplane petrol lighter	7	7	■ ■	50-80	80-130
chrome elephant, 'Perpetual Match'	7	7	■ ■	50-80	80-130
Dunhill	8	7	■ ■	750-1000	1200-1600
Ronson 'Cocktail Bar'	6	7	■ ■ ■	250-500	400-800
Tea and coffee services					
pottery tea set with chrome covers to teapot, milk jug and sugar basin	6	7	■	35-40 set	55-60
silver cube teapot	7	8	■ ■	400-800	640-1280
Watches					
cocktail watch, brilliants and baguette cut onyx in platinum	8	8	■ ■	700-1000	1120-1600
cocktail watch, marcasite and silver on silver bracelet	7	7	■	80-250	130-400
cocktail watch, paste and silver on silver bracelet	7	7	■	150-300	240-480
enamelled fob watch, enamelled pin	8	8	■ ■	300-500	480-800
geometric enamelled holder	8	8	■ ■	500-600	800-1000

Qualities on a scale 1-10   ■ Rare   ■ ■ Very rare   ■ ■ ■ Extremely rare

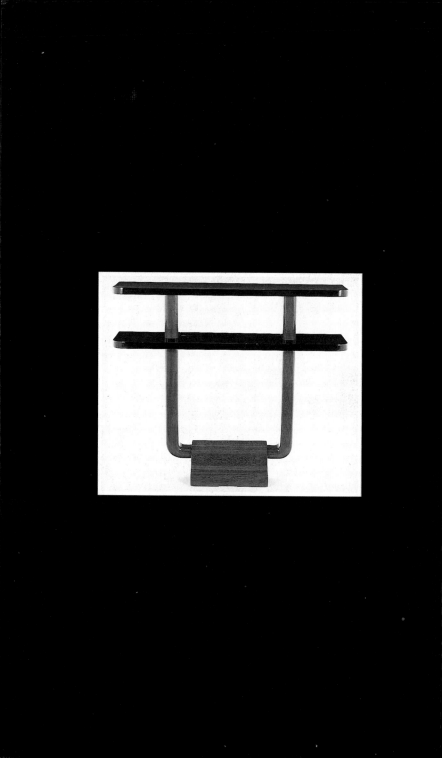

CHAPTER SIX

FURNITURE
AND
TEXTILES

Console table with lacquered shelves
and palisander base. Sold: Sotheby's,
Monaco, 19/10/86. Price: 7770FF.

**Mirror with chromed metal
stand**
Height: 28cm
William Harvey & Hilary Conquy,
N6 Antiquarius, London
Price: £68

As with every area of design between the Wars, furniture was affected by the implications of mass production. This is not to say that every designer worked for the mass market, but the 'machine aesthetic' — with its clean lines and rejection of surface decoration — influenced the great craftsman-designers like Ruhlmann as well as furniture companies which had hitherto found their inspiration in the shapes and motifs of the traditional past. The best mass-produced furniture of the period is that which capitalized on its machine origins by using manmade materials — plywood, chromed steel and plastics. In the end, what links the crafted and luxurious Art Deco of the early twenties with the Modernist 'machined' style of the thirties is the assimilation and development of a series of ideas in response to a rapidly changing society on both sides of the Atlantic and to the advent of machine production on a large scale.

EARLY ART DECO FURNITURE

The origins of the Art Deco style in furniture can be traced to the beginning of the twentieth century and specifically to Germany and Austria. The Wiener Werkstätte was founded in 1903 in Vienna with Josef Hoffmann and Koloman (Kolo) Moser as artistic directors. The ideas of the early Werkstätte are probably best expressed in their most important commission, the Brussels mansion for Adolphe Stoclet, begun in 1904. In a city which contained some of the most exuberant examples of Art Nouveau the Palais Stoclet must have seemed almost austere, the impression of austerity arising from its mainly monochrome exterior and the disciplined, geometric division of its surfaces. In fact the building and its interiors are extremely luxurious; Hoffman and Moser were given a free hand to choose the best materials, so the walls were clad in marble and the furniture was constructed from the most costly hardwoods and finely treated leathers, while the fittings were made with 'the best-quality glass and metals.

It was this precise combination of luxury and geometric discipline which impressed the French couturier Paul Poiret when he visited the Palais Stoclet in 1910. That Poiret should undertake a visit to Brussels specifically to see Hoffmann's building is in itself significant. French designers had encountered the work of the Deutscher Werkbund at the Salon d'Automne in Paris in 1910, and to many of them it seemed to offer a real alternative to Art Nouveau and a direction forward, combining as it did the geometric 'machine' style with a strong element of classicism.

On his return to Paris, Poiret established the Atelier Martine, which produced both fabrics and furniture; the latter were particularly influenced by Werkstätte design but with an additional lightness of touch. The unity of design which Poiret had noted in the Palais Stoclet was echoed in the products of his own establishment together with simple lines and basic forms.

Jacques-Emile Ruhlmann, already an established furniture designer, began as early as 1913 to produce pieces which were richly luxurious in their materials but which had a disciplined subtlety of shape and decoration which sets them apart from Art Nouveau.

THE NEW FURNITURE OF THE TWENTIES

There are certain pieces of furniture which are uniquely Art Deco and which make their first appearance in the twenties. The cocktail cabinet is an example, created to accommodate the large number of accessories needed to make the fashionable alcoholic concoctions of the decade. (America is credited with the invention of the cocktail; the legend tells us that mixed drinks were evolved to hide the taste of bootleg alcohol. The story may well be apocryphal but it is certainly true that the classic cocktail recipes all come from the States.)

Dressing tables also became important in the twenties. A large range of beauty products were appearing on the market, often stylishly packaged to be displayed. The dressing table provided display and storage space, and a place to apply make-up. Before the War such an item of furniture was simply not necessary;

by the end of the twenties a 'ladies' dressing table' was part of even the cheapest mass-produced bedroom suite. For the designer this new object gave an ideal opportunity to use essentially modern forms and materials – circular mirrors which contrasted with rectangular bases, chrome and glass which could be combined with wood, and so on.

Epstein & Goldbart cocktail cabinet, sycamore veneered
Height: 153.6cm
Sold: Christie's South Kensington, London, 19/9/86
Price: £550

111

Cocktail cabinet
Height: 160cm
Sold: Sotheby's, London, 16/5/86
Price: £605

The sophisticated technology in the glass-manufacturing industries on both sides of the Atlantic at the end of the twenties made possible the production of a vast range of coloured and textured glass. By the thirties the mirrored interior in both public places and private homes had become fashionable, as had plate-glass furniture and pieces covered with mirror glass. Plate glass was a material used by the modern movement, often with chrome, and most glass and metal furniture bears all the stylistic hallmarks of Modernism even if, like Denham MacLaren's tables and chairs, it was made for a strictly fashionable market. Mirrored pieces on the other hand were essen-tially 'voguish', their glamour often residing in their novelty rather than in any real craftsmanship. The life of a peach-glass cocktail cabinet or a mirror-mosaic table was short for two reasons: the inherent fragility of the material made damage inevit-able, and the high fashion aspect of such pieces carried with it the cer-tainty of obsolescence. To mass manufacturers mirror glass was a useful and profitable development because it could be used to cover a cheaply constructed carcass and give an immediate impression of mod-ernity; mirrored furniture persisted on the mass market long after it had ceased to be made elsewhere.

FRENCH FURNITURE AND TEXTILES

It was certainly in Paris that the Art Deco style in furniture first became readily identifiable. By the time of the 1925 Exhibition of the Decorative Arts it was the accepted high style, at least in Europe. Many American de-signers looked slightly askance at the developments in France. What was acceptable in architecture in that country was less acceptable in the home, and the continent that was even then producing the great sky-scrapers of the twenties regarded Art Deco furniture as 'modish', 'novel' or even 'vicious'. Despite this, French Art Deco was imported into the United States at the beginning of the decade, but it was sold only through fashionable and very expensive shops.

Mass production of furniture was not a consideration at the time of the 1925 Exhibition, although several interior design companies were estab-lished to provide the middle-class market with fashionable furniture and textiles. Stores like the Galeries Lafayette opened their own decorating departments and employed a design director to co-ordinate the objects sold there. Those who could not afford the work of the great craftsman-designers could still furn-

French dressing table, burr veneered
Height: 136cm
Sold: Sotheby's, London, 16/5/86
Price: £715

ish their homes in the new, integrated style of the ensemble, and with furniture which was clearly in the modern manner.

Artists like Ruhlmann, Jules Leleu and Jean Dunand produced objects which were beautifully made and from materials which were rare, often exotic and by their nature expensive. The work of such master craftsman-designers was never intended for any but the richest patrons, but their influence was far reaching. Ruhlmann's use of beautifully grained woods to define the geometric surfaces of his furniture was an inspiration to the design companies and ultimately to the furniture industry. Dunand's lacquer work was widely imitated and contributed to the acceptance of painted furniture. In many ways their posi-

Chair by Dominique
Height: 77cm
Sold: Sotheby's, London, 16/5/86
Price (pair): £880

Side table veneered in zebrawood
Height: 74.5cm
Sold: Sotheby's, London, 16/5/86
Price: £990

tion can be compared to that of the great couturiers of the twenties; they generated ideas and even though the objects they produced were exclusive and costly the ideas behind them had widespread influence.

The designs displayed at the Exhibition of 1925 reveal an astonishing range of sources; much of Paul Follot's work for the Pomone studio drew on eighteenth-century French furniture for its motifs, as did Dufrêne's for La Maîtrise. Ruhlmann borrowed from Empire design whereas Dunand took both his shapes and his technique of lacquering from the Far East. What unites these disparate sources is the modification of silhouette and detail into simplified forms inspired by 'the machine'. In every case the furniture is distinctly modern.

A further source of inspiration came from 'primitive' art. After the First World War the influence of African tribal art began to appear in furniture design, soon to be joined by those of pre-Columbian American art and of ancient Egypt. Each of these cultures provided furniture designers with a repertoire of forms based almost entirely on geometric and abstract shapes which bore little resemblance to any of the accepted traditions of mainstream European design. Marcel Coard produced furniture which is evidently inspired by both African and Egyptian art and is often executed in strong, slightly barbaric colours; Pierre Legrain made pieces which were based directly on tribal designs; and Eileen Gray, a British designer who moved to France in 1907, produced stools, couches and other items of furniture for the couturiers Jacques Doucet and Suzanne Talbot, using forms taken from dynastic Egyptian sources.

In textile design the Cubist/Primitive influence was particularly important. For example, the Compagnie des Arts Français exhibited furniture in 1925 which was upholstered in a fabric that was a Cubist formalization of a traditional eighteenth-century pastoral tapestry. The painter Raoul Dufy, among others, was designing fabrics for the Atelier Martine which were printed in strong colours, particularly indigo, and given names like 'Africa'. The abstract shapes of 'primitive' art were particularly well adapted to carpet and rug design because they emphasize the flat surface. At the beginning of the twenties the textile designer Bruno da Silva Bruhns was using Berber motifs on rugs and later adapted the strong colours and geometric shapes of other African

HMV electric fire
Height: 37.5cm
David Rayner, N4/5 Antiquarius,
London
Price: £85

textiles in his floor coverings. By the end of the decade the same influences appeared in textiles produced for the mass market.

BRITISH FURNITURE AND TEXTILES

The British pavilion at the 1925 Exhibition was poorly received by the French critics. After allowing for a degree of anglophobia in their criticism it must be admitted that they were right in remarking that the designs shown were old fashioned and out of tune with the new spirit so evident elsewhere in the Exhibition. On the whole British designers had retreated into a kind of historical cosiness with reproduction 'Tudorbethan' remaining a clear favourite with the general public. However, Ambrose Heal, whose company was closely associated with the Arts and Crafts movement, had been a founder member in 1915 of the Design and 115

**French walnut-veneered
dining room suite**
Height (chair): 118cm
Sold: Phillips, London, 21/10/86
Price (9 pieces): £572

Industries Association, and he was concerned even then by the lack of cooperation between the craftsman-designer and industry in Britain, and by the apparent reluctance of either to move into the twentieth century. As a retailer Heal was able to commission work to be sold in his shop and could thus encourage furniture and textile designers who were exploring new ideas in their work. He opened his Mansard Gallery at the London shop specifically to show modern designs to the public. Some of the furniture shown there was mass produced, some craftsman-built; all of it showed a clear affinity of style with Continental design. Heal

himself combined Arts and Crafts techniques with Art Deco shapes in the pieces marketed as the 'Signed Edition Series'.

Like Heal, the craftsman-designer Gordon Russell was able to adapt to the new forms, and made furniture which combined traditional materials with clean geometric shapes. In the thirties both Russell and Heal turned their attention to mass production and manmade materials, and marketed furniture built in steel and laminated wood.

Serge Chermayeff directed the Modern Art Studio for Waring and Gillow in London which was organized in the same way as the Parisian department-store studios. His own simple but dramatic designs, with coordinated floor coverings, were sold there with modern furniture and textiles by other designers.

Betty Joel sold French-influenced furniture from her own shop in Knightsbridge from 1919, when her company was formed. Throughout the twenties her designs were manifestly de luxe, often heavily upholstered in strongly coloured satins and teamed with signed rugs. Later in the decade, and afterwards in the thirties, her work became simpler and more geometric, and she made use of industrially produced plywood laminates and other manmade materials. The Rowley Gallery also sold stylish furniture which, with its decorative inlay and tasselled handles, showed a Continental influence.

The single area in which Britain kept pace with France was that of textile design. Companies like Arundel Clarke, Allan Walton and Tamesa Fabrics sold original designs commissioned from their teams of artists. Allan Walton sold a range of fabrics designed by the French painter and textile designer Sonia Delaunay, who produced prints for them in her characteristic clear, bright colours and geometric shapes. The Edinburgh Weavers and the Wilton Royal Carpet factory also employed design teams; Edinburgh Weavers were particularly concerned to produce a range of floor coverings which would coordinate with the modern interior. With this in mind Marion Dorn designed a range in restrained colours with a strong, Modernist motif. Both she and her husband, the graphic artist E. McKnight-Kauffer, developed a style of rug clearly influenced by Modernist paintings and lacking the traditional elements associated with decorative rugs; there is no fringed edging or patterned border. Like paintings, these rugs were intended to be significant features of an interior, rather than just an accessory.

FURNITURE AND TEXTILES IN AMERICA

The United States did not contribute a pavilion to the 1925 Exhibition. It was felt that the country was producing nothing in the way of original design except in its architecture and industrial design. Paul Frankl, who wrote a scalding criticism of the state of American decorative arts in 1928, was one of the few designers in the United States who recognized the importance of what was happening in France. It was American architecture that first showed the stylistic elements associated with Art Deco – the Chrysler building and the Chanin building were both constructed with geometrical decorative elements on their exteriors and with coordinated

Carpet

361 x 278cm

Sold: Sotheby's, London, 19/12/86

Price: £638

interior design. Even so, Art Deco as a style for the domestic interior was still regarded with some suspicion. Frank Lloyd-Wright had been creating houses and the furnishings for them since the beginning of the century in a style which had its roots in the Arts and Crafts movement. The Robie House, for example, built in 1908 in Chicago, was conceived as a complete design including the furniture, textiles and mechanical services, lighting, heating and so on. This unity of design can be linked with Continental ideas, as can Lloyd-

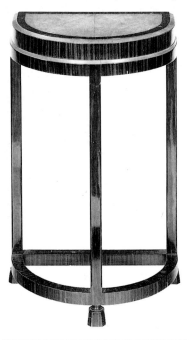

Heal's calamander and shagreen console table
Height: 72cm
Sold: Sotheby's, London, 16/5/86
Price: £770

Wright's use of simplified geometric shapes, but he too was less than enthusiastic about French design and was concerned as to how appropriate it was to America.

Frankl's furniture in the twenties shows a clear progression from pieces designed with a French influence to something more markedly American. His 'Skyscraper' pieces are interesting for two reasons: he believed that an interior should be in keeping with its surroundings; and the 'Skyscraper' units reflect the shapes of the urban landscape. They are also multi-purpose, performing the combined functions of bookcase, storage space and display shelves. They were designed with a restricted living space in mind: Frankl was aware that urban living, particularly, involved smaller rooms than those in traditional houses, and although his furniture was hand-built and therefore costly it did influence mass production in the later twenties and the thirties.

Cranbrook Academy, which was founded in the twenties in Michigan and had as its architect, designer and director the Scandinavian Eliel Saarinen, is sometimes referred to as 'the American Bauhaus'. However erroneous that description may be it is certainly true that the designs produced in the studios and workshops there were influential and in tune with the Modernist tenets of unified design. Saarinen's own furniture has a linear elegance which can be traced back to Josef Hoffmann's designs for the Palais Stoclet, and he was quite able to use new materials while remaining faithful to the principles of craftsmanship taught at the Academy.

Saarinen's wife Loja directed the textile studio at Cranbrook. In the

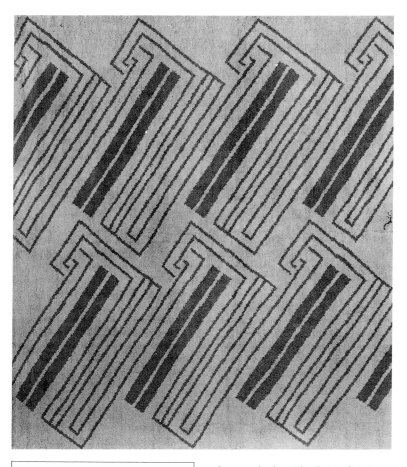

Carpet
272 × 248cm
Sold: Sotheby's, London, 19/12/86
Price: £495

who worked with Loja Saarinen, adapted Aztec and Mayan decorative and symbolic shapes for her hand-woven rugs.

GERMAN FURNITURE AND THE BAUHAUS INFLUENCE

late twenties her designs were clearly based on Peruvian woven fabrics; the carpets she made for Cranbrook incorporate the rectangular patterns and the colouring of South American blankets. Maja Andersson Wirde,

Like America, Germany contributed nothing to the Paris Exhibition but the reasons were political rather than because Germany felt it had nothing to show. Despite this absence French designers were aware

119

of developments in that country, particularly those at the Bauhaus. From its first years in Weimar the Bauhaus was producing successful designs in its studio classrooms, particularly in the areas of textile and metalwork, but it was after its move to the industrial city of Dessau in 1925 that it began to make a serious impact on international design. One of Dessau's stipulations for accepting the school was that its designs should be able to be mass produced at a reasonable price. Walter Gropius, the founder, was more than willing to accept this condition because it accorded with his own ideas, and from 1925 until the school closed for ever in 1933 it produced designs that were suitable for machine production.

In the furniture workshops staff and students began to explore the possibilities of chromed tubular steel, and prototypes were made by Ludwig Mies van der Rohe and Marcel Breuer. Today we regard many Bauhaus designs as 'classics' but at the time they received a mixed reception in both Europe and America, the usual criticism being that the furniture was clinical and utilitarian. Nevertheless, by the end of the twenties some aspects of Bauhaus design and of the designs of other Modernists like the Swiss architect Le Corbusier were adopted even by more traditional designers. In France Ruhlmann modified his designs to include metals and plain geometric surfaces. In America furniture makers like Donald Deskey and Kem Weber adapted the 'machine style'

Eavestaff 'Minipiano' and stool
Width: 129cm
Sold: Sotheby's, London, 16/5/86
Price: £682

and turned it into something more luxurious and chic. Deskey's furniture for S.L. Rothafel's private office in Radio City, part of the Rockefeller Centre in New York, is constructed entirely from chromed metal with the joints clearly stressed in the Bauhaus manner. There is in the end, however, only a superficial resemblance between Bauhaus-influenced Art Deco and the actual products of the school itself. At the end of the twenties Modernism was still being used as a style for objects which were expensive and which were not mass produced in any real sense.

MASS-PRODUCED FURNITURE

The Depression changed the nature of furniture design on both sides of the Atlantic for two basic reasons. Furniture in the de luxe tradition was simply no longer appropriate to the new mood of society and, on a more pragmatic level, the old market no longer existed. The thirties saw both the emergence of new companies which mass produced in a real sense and also a new role for the designer. It had been understood for some time in America that a well-designed product sold better than one which was less visually attractive. The automobile industry was possibly the first to appreciate this fact fully and the

---

Leather upholstered 3-piece suite
Height: 80cm
Sold: Sotheby's, London, 16/5/86
Price: £528

---

relationship between the designer and industry had been vigorously encouraged in the States from the mid-twenties.

Britain and France were late in coming to terms with this idea; in fact it was not until 1935 and the 'British Art in Industry' Exhibition that there was any concerted effort in England to encourage designers to think in terms of mass production, particularly in the furniture industry. Even so, stylish Art Deco furniture was certainly being produced for the popular market in the second half of the twenties. Most of it was made in unfortunate imitation of French de luxe, constructed from cheap materials and sometimes cellulose-painted to imitate lacquer. In the early thirties some attempt was made to add elements of Modernism with the grafting of chromed 'extras' on to an existing design. A surprising number of these pieces still survive and it is occasionally possible to find one which is very stylish and a credit to its anonymous designer.

121

The companies which approached the business of mass production in the most realistic way were often ones which had been in existence for some time, making furniture which fell outside the category of 'fashionable' design. Thonet, for example, had been making bentwood furniture since the mid-nineteenth century for the mass market. In 1929 it increased its range to include tubular steel pieces and employed Le Corbusier to design for it. The result of this relationship between designer and industry was a range of furniture which was stylish, practical and able to be manufactured at sensible prices.

> **Dining room suite in walnut, maple and chromed steel**
> Width (sideboard): 130cm
> Sold: Bonham's, London, 27/6/86
> Price (6 pieces): £715

The French company DIM (Décoration Intérieure Moderne), founded in 1919 by René Joubert, was the first firm in that country to produce tubular steel furniture for the popular market. Both Thonet and DIM products were being imported into Britain at the end of the twenties and, more importantly, were being seen in places which were luxurious and chic. It was apparently the presence of a tubular steel chair by either Thonet or DIM in the foyer of the Strand Palace Hotel that induced the English industrial company Tube Investments Ltd to begin manufacturing furniture under the name PEL (Practical Equipment Ltd). PEL took the very sensible step of inviting the architect and designer Wells Coates to produce some prototypes for it and much of its subsequent output was influenced by his ideas. PEL products were by no means the cheapest mass-produced furniture; in 1937 the price of its tubular steel and walnut

Wooden box
10 × 8cm
Malcolm Haslam, London
Price: £20

table could have bought a complete bedroom suite from a company like Oetzmann and Co. which made inexpensive furniture for the mass market. But it was stylish and well made and was recognized in its time as the essence of practical, go-ahead modernity. This perhaps accounts for its unprecedented success as a piece of boardroom furniture in the 1930s.

The company with which Wells Coates is most strongly associated is Isokon, which produced both architecture and furniture. It was Isokon that popularized plywood in England, although it was already being used in Scandinavia by the designer Alvar Aalto for furniture produced by his company, Artek. Many manufacturers who mass produced furniture used plywood as a substitute for the 'real thing'. The

development of a wide range of finishes, including a metallic effect, was a real advantage to such companies. Neither Artek or Isokon used plywood as a substitute but designed specifically for it, exploiting the flexibility of the material which could be bent through a complex series of curves to fit even the contours of the human body. In 1935 Marcel Breuer, during a brief stay in England, was employed as consultant designer to Isokon, for which he designed the 'Long Chair'. Constructed from plywood on a beech frame, it is both comfortable and almost sculptural in its elegance. Later in the thirties Gerald Sumner designed domestic furniture for the company which continued the idea of sculptural form; in the trolley he designed for Isokon the smooth, streamlined forms of later Art Deco are particularly well demonstrated.

In America too there was a realistic approach to the business of 123 producing reasonably priced furniture for the mass market in the thirties. Industrial designers such as Raymond Loewy and Norman Bel Geddes included tubular steel and glass furniture in their interiors. Product designer Henry Dreyfuss also used the newly developed Formica in conjunction with chromed metal in the interiors of the *Twentieth Century Ltd* express train. In the end, however, it was probably the designer Russel Wright who did most to bring Modernist design to the public in America. His range 'Modern Living', which included furniture constructed from maple in solid, simple shapes, coordinated furnishing fabrics, rugs, curtains and lighting, sold through the department store Macy's and was an immensely popular success. Wright succeeded in bringing to the American public one of the most basic Art Deco ideas, that of the integrated interior. Although his work is identifiably American it can be compared with the products of the Union des Artistes Modernes in France which was founded in 1930 by René Hebst and other designers. While not comparable in price terms the Union's designs show an awareness of the needs of the public in the thirties – a need for furniture designed for smaller spaces and a corresponding need for pieces which coordinate. By the end of the thirties the idea of the complete interior was no longer a matter of expressing elegant taste; it was rather a realistic way of coping with the restricted space in modern houses and apartments.

COLLECTING FURNITURE AND TEXTILES

The craftsman-made pieces of furni-

Plywood armchair designed by Alvar Aalto
Height: 76cm
Sold: Sotheby's, London, 16/5/86
Price (pair): £330

ture and textiles of the twenties are rare and correspondingly expensive. Much of the range produced by the French design studios like Pomone is also difficult to obtain; smaller items of interior design, like the wooden boxes made for cigarettes, are more available. The work of a designer like Betty Joel who did not produce exclusive pieces but nonetheless made furniture which had a clear identity is usually reasonably priced.

Furniture which was designed for mass production is still obtainable; pieces by Thonet, Isokon, Artek, PEL and DIM can be found in the large salerooms and sometimes in nonspecialist 'old furniture' shops. But much of the tubular steel furniture bought by companies to furnish their offices and boardrooms in the thirties was literally thrown out in the sixties and unfortunately a great deal of it was simply destroyed. The fact that the pieces which have survived are still in fair condition is a tribute to the standards of manufacture of the period. PEL, Thonet and DIM products can be identified by the makers' labels. It is worth remembering that Breuer's designs for Isokon have been reproduced since the sixties, as have Le Corbusier's for Thonet and Mies van der Rohe's 'Barcelona' chair. Russel Wright's 'Modern Living' range can still be found but it is now being extensively collected, as are his ceramics, and both are becoming expensive and are virtually unobtainable outside America.

Undoubtedly the largest area which remains to be explored by the collector is that of furniture and textiles made in imitation of the unique originals. In the twenties particularly there was a large middle-class market which admired the products of the studios while not being able to afford them. It is possible to find well-made and stylish furniture and floor coverings made in 'the manner' of a particular designer or design group and produced for the middle market in less costly materials and with a minimum of hand finishing. Mass production need not imply 'cheap and nasty'.

Isokon chaise longue designed by Marcel Breuer
Height: 80cm
Sold: Sotheby's, London, 16/5/86
Price: £990

Object	Quality of manufacture	Quality of design and/or decoration	Rarity	Price (£)	Price ($)
Aalto, Alvar					
laminate chair for Finmar	8	9	■ ■	700-750	1120-1200
pair of laminate chairs, angular arms	8	8	■ ■	300-400	480-640
Anon.					
bedroom suite (bed, dressing table, 2 wardrobes), maple veneer	6	6	■ ■	350-400	560-640
bedroom suite (bed, wardrobe, dressing table, stool and chest), green cellulose paint on plywood with metal handles	4	5	■ ■	75-150	120-240
box, mirror glass	6	6	■ ■	15-40	20-60
boxes, wooden, geometric designs in various woods	6	6	■	10-30	20-50
cabinet, cocktail, chrome and sycamore, Modernist	7	7	■ ■	700-750	1120-1200
cabinet, cocktail, sycamore with carved panels, imported from China	8	7	■ ■	300-350	480-560
cabinet, display, drum-shaped on curved feet, glass front	6	6	■	80-170	130-270
cabinet, display, with stepped sides and glass front, walnut	6	6	■	60-150	100-240
cabinets, pair of bedside, rosewood	7	6	■ ■	350-400	560-640
cigarette box, laquered, geometric design in manner of Dunand	7	7	■ ■	50-150	80-240
desk, rosewood	7	8	■	950-1000	1520-1600
dining chairs, leather (set of 4)	6	6	■ ■	100-160	160-260
dining room suite (9 pieces including 6 chairs)	6	6	■	550-650	880-1040
dining room suite (table and 10 chairs)	7	7	■ ■	900-1000	1400-1600
dining table, walnut, maple and tubular steel, with 4 chairs	7	7	■	700-800	1120-1280

Qualities on a scale 1-10   ■ Rare   ■ ■ Very rare   ■ ■ ■ Extremely rare

Object	Quality of manufacture	Quality of design and/or decoration	Rarity	Price (£)	Price ($)
Anon. contd					
dressing table, burr veneered, Modernist	7	7	■ ■	700-750	1120-1200
dressing table, tubular steel, glass	7	6	■ ■	350-400	560-640
mirror in sunburst shape, green glass alternating with mirror glass, clock at centre	6	6	■ ■ ■	50-80	80-130
mirror, hall, in painted wood, style of Mall et Stevens	7	8	■	750-800	1200-1280
mirror, wall, with shagreen frame	7	7	■ ■	150-300	240-480
mirror, fan-shaped, with coloured glass at the sides	6	6	■ ■ ■	40-80	60-130
nursery furniture (wardrobe, bed and chest with mirror), wood painted with yacht design – mirror yacht-shaped	7	8	■	300-450	480-720
pedestal table, mirror glass, possibly James Clark Ltd	6	6	■ ■	200-400	320-640
rug, Modernist	6	6	■ ■	30-150	50-240
screen, painted fabric, in manner of the Compagnie des Arts Français	7	7	■ ■	250-350	400-560
shelving unit, painted metal	6	6	■ ■	150-200	240-320
side table, zebra wood	8	8	■ ■	950-1000	1520-1600
three piece suite, leather	7	5	■ ■	500-700	800-1120
trolley, cocktail, chrome and glass	6	6	■ ■ ■	80-200	130-320
Breuer, Marcel					
long chair for Isokon	8	9	■ ■	800-1000+	1280-1600+
Clarke, Arundell					
armchair upholstered in dark blue fabric	7	7	■ ■	400	640
chair, brown moquette, copy of Arundell Clarke	5	5	■ ■	30-60	50-100

Qualities on a scale 1-10 ■ Rare ■ ■ Very rare ■ ■ ■ Extremely rare **127**

Object	Quality of manufacture	Quality of design and/or decoration	Rarity	Price (£)	Price ($)
Dominique					
pair of bergères	7	7	■ ■	750-900	1200-1440
Epstein & Goldbart					
mahogany veneered cocktail cabinet	8	8	■ ■	500-550	750-880
Frankl, Paul					
settee in fruitwood	7	7	■ ■	850-1000+	1360-1600+
Heal's					
console table, calamander and shagreen	8	8	■	750-800	1200-1280
bedroom suite (bed, 2 wardrobes and 2 dressing tables), limed oak	7	7	■ ■	600-700	960-1120
desk, chrome and enamelled metal	7	7	■ ■	150-200	240-320
desk with fan-shaped stepped top, oak	7	7	■ ■	300-350	480-560
Hermann Ltd					
extending table, walnut with chrome legs	6	5	■ ■ ■	80-150	130-240
sideboard *en suite* with above	6	5	■ ■ ■	80-150	130-240
Joel, Betty					
armchair, sycamore and cerise satin	7	6	■ ■	150-200	240-320
cabinet, satinwood, on chest	7	7	■ ■	420-500	670-800
cabinet, walnut, on chest	6	6	■ ■	150-200	240-320
chest of drawers, mahogany	7	7	■ ■	550-600	880-960
day bed, sycamore and cerise satin	7	6	■ ■	400-650	640-1040
dressing table, laminated wood with ivory handles and circular mirror	8	8	■ ■	400-500	640-800
rug	7	8	■	500-800	800-1280

Qualities on a scale 1-10   ■ Rare   ■ ■ Very rare   ■ ■ ■ Extremely rare

Object	Quality of manufacture	Quality of design and/or decoration	Rarity	Price (£)	Price ($)
Le Corbusier					
'Le Grand Confort' chair, manufactured by Cassina, 1975	8	9	■	500-600	800-960
Mies van der Rohe					
pair Barcelona chairs, polished steel	8	9	■ ■	950-1000+	1520-1600+
pair Barcelona chairs, chromed metal	7	9	■ ■	700-800	1120-1280
pair cantilevered chairs for Knoll International	8	9	■	80-110	130-180
PEL					
chromed steel bed	7	7	■ ■	200-350	320-560
dining/board-room table, ebonized wood and chrome	7	8	■ ■	600-700	960-11200
Ponti, Gio					
table	7	8	■	900-1000	1440-1600
Rashke					
3-piece suite	7	7	■ ■	600-700	960-1120
Rowley					
screen, four leaves with marquetry panel on each	8	8	■ ■ ■	540-600	860-1000
Royal Wilton					
rug	7	8	■ ■	200-500	320-800
rug, Marion Dorn	7	8	■	500-800	800-1280
Summers, Gerald					
laminate chair for Simple Furniture	8	9	■ ■	500-700	800-1120
Widdicomb Co., John					
desk, chrome and hardwood	7	7	■ ■	300-400	480-640

Qualities on a scale 1-10   ■ Rare   ■ ■ Very rare   ■ ■ ■ Extremely rare

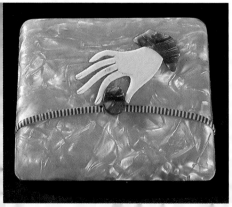

CHAPTER SEVEN

PLASTICS

Celluloid cigarette case. John Jesse &
Irina Laski, London. Price: £50.

The decades between the First and Second World Wars marked the 'coming of age' of synthetic materials and saw their wide application to a vast range of consumer items. The term 'plastic' means, among other things, 'capable of being moulded'; although synthetics are by no means the only materials to which this applies, by the twenties the term 'plastic' was used exclusively and generically to describe manmade materials which were by then being manufactured and sold under a variety of trade names.

Art Deco was a style which was well able to accommodate plastics, and to use them for their own particular properties: their bright colours, their adaptability, and the way in which they could be combined with other, more traditional, materials to produce a look which was completely new. In the thirties, and most particularly in America, plastics were widely used in the newest areas of design and were actively promoted with competitions like the 'Modern Plastics' award of 1936 (won by the Toledo Scale Co. with a weighing machine housed in pure white urea formaldehyde).

NATURAL PLASTICS

Although most of the plastics used between the Wars were manmade it is worth mentioning the 'natural' plastics which occasionally appear in the Art Deco period.

Horn is a natural plastic in that it can be softened by boiling or soaking it in an alkaline solution and can then be moulded, pressed or inlaid. Although the first patent for a screw press to make horn combs was taken out in America in 1818, decorative hair-slides (barettes) and Spanish combs were still being made this way in the twenties. Small horn boxes were also made in Italy, intended as dressing-table accessories. These were often incised with a design on the lid, usually of formalized flowers. Horn can also be ground and then compression-moulded into buttons, buckles and so on; the Lawson Moulding Co. in the States was still making buttons for the garment industry in this way at the beginning of the twenties.

Tortoiseshell, usually from the Hawksbill turtle, is another natural plastic. It can be laminated in thin sheets which, when heated, can be stamped, pressed and moulded. By the end of the nineteenth century it had been superseded by the much cheaper celluloid, which can be coloured in imitation of tortoiseshell.

Amber, a natural resin, was heated and moulded in the twenties to make beads and other decorative items.

Pair of candlesticks with 'candles' in cast phenolic
Height: 20cm
John Jesse & Irina Laski, London
Price: £30

The amber which forms the mouthpiece of the cigarette holders that were such a fashionable accessory at that time is often 'Ambroid', made from scraps and fragments of the material which were melted down and moulded.

Shellac, produced from the secretions of insects which live on acacia trees, was one of the most widely used of the natural plastics until after the Second World War, although from the beginning of the century its use tended to be industrial rather than decorative. It was used as a binder for other compounds, a laminating compound, an insulating material and as a coating for wood and steel. It was particularly important to the expanding electrical industry because of its insulating properties. Until Thomas Edison began using Bakelite for records in 1910, shellac was the only material capable of taking moulding fine enough for good-quality recordings. The labels of the Italian company Fonotopia of Milan (which existed before the First World War) depict the press used to make shellac records operated by a generously proportioned and languid muse.

Vulcanite (hard rubber) and bitumen were two natural compounds much used in the twenties. Vulcanite was used by the Waterman fountain pen company for the barrels and caps of pens which were then fitted with gold or gold-plated bands and clips. Such pens are usually black or a slightly marbled brown, and marked with the maker's name. Bitumen continued to be used because of its heat-resistant properties; it made an ideal material for the handles of the new lightweight cooking utensils which were replacing cast iron pots in the modern kitchen.

Celluloid box
Diameter: 12cm
John Jesse & Irina Laski, London
Price: £50

SEMI-SYNTHETIC PLASTICS

Many of the semi-synthetic plastics are derived from wood cellulose; one of the earliest, 'collodion', was used by the textile industry as a waterproofing agent and as a laminate for detachable collars. Later the cosmetic companies were to manufacture nail varnishes with a collodion base. When extruded to form fine fibre collodion became the first synthetic silk. Called Chardonnet silk, after its inventor, the fabric was instantly popular despite the fact that it was lethally inflammable. From 1884, when it first appeared, until 1892, when rayon was developed, the market for Chardonnet silk increased steadily to the point where 3,500lb were being manufactured each day.

The first viscose rayon stockings were marketed in 1910, and other forms of rayon, also derived from cellulose, were being sold in the thirties under the trade names 'Celanese' and 'Tricel'. Cellophane, a

133

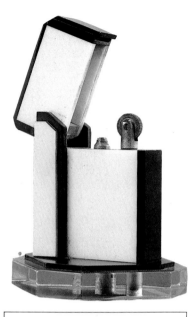

Exhibition in London where he was awarded medals for his decorative moulded combs, buttons and knife handles. The major disadvantage of Parkesine was that its 'fillers', natural fibres used to bulk the compound, restricted its colour range.

In the twenties Xylonite, a white version of Parkesine, was used extensively by manufacturers such as Halex in the production of dressing-table sets. Some of these are imitation ivory, some are more inventive in their use of the material, combining colours and utilizing shapes which are characteristic of the

viscose and glycerol compound, was developed in 1912. The original producers, La Cellophane Société Anonyme, of France, sold rights to the material to Du Pont of America who developed a method of waterproofing the film, thereby increasing its commercial potential. From 1926 Cellophane became one of the staple materials for packaging on both sides of the Atlantic. In the thirties it was woven into fabrics by Schiaparelli and used as appliqué by her and by dressmakers who copied her designs.

Parkesine was the trade name of the first commercially mouldable pyroxylin; its inventor exhibited several items manufactured from the compound at the 1862 International

period. Halex produced a set shortly after the discovery of the tomb of Tutankhamun, which was coloured *eau-de-Nil* and moulded in the fashionable 'Egyptian' shapes. Some of the first plastic handbags were made from Xylonite. These accessories, which date from the twenties, were often hand-coloured, decorated with silk tassels and fitted inside with a plastic-backed mirror and a matching lipstick tube.

In America the Celluloid Manufacturing Co. was founded by Hyatt in 1871. The possibilities of the material were immediately recognized by the toy industry, and dolls with celluloid heads were made by 1873 using a process called 'blow moulding'. By the twenties toys made entirely by blow moulding celluloid were being exported to the States and to Britain from Japan. 'Kewpie' dolls and 'Kelly' dolls (weighted in the base to rock from side to side) are the most readily identifiable as dolls made in the twenties.

Like Xylonite, celluloid was also used in the manufacture of a range of small-scale objects. At the end of the nineteenth century it became popular as imitation tortoiseshell: boxes, book covers and hair combs were made at a fraction of the cost of laminated tortoiseshell. Later, celluloid powder boxes, dressing-table sets, traveller's toilet cases fitted with soap box and toothbrush holder, napkin rings, handbag frames (the latter without a maker's name but often marked 'French') and various buttons were made, often in imitation tortoiseshell.

Celluloid was frequently used in conjunction with metal in the twenties and thirties: dressing-table boxes, for example, were made with chromed feet or lids, buttons and buckles from steel covered in coloured celluloid sheets and hairbrushes from celluloid over metal with a characteristically Art Deco pattern – a stepped pyramid shape, for example, or a sunburst described in metal cut-out over the plastic. It is worth remembering that Art Deco shapes persisted in the design of plastic accessories after the Second World War. The soap boxes in traveller's sets retained diagonally cut and fluted corners, and dressing-table sets retained a streamlined, stepped silhouette well into the fifties.

Of the semi-synthetic plastics, casein, a milk protein-based compound, is probably the most beautiful. Its use was restricted to small-scale and mainly decorative objects because it had poor moisture resistance and a tendency to wear badly.

Cast phenolic Thermos flask
Height: 27cm
John Jesse & Irina Laski, London
Price: £30

135

Marketed under various names (Erinoid in Britain, and Aladdanite in America), casein was made in a number of finishes from solid colours to a translucent 'flaked' effect reminiscent of mother of pearl. It could be used to imitate amber, ebony, agate and malachite as well as the more usual tortoiseshell and ivory. Erinoid was the standard material for manufacturing knitting needles from 1918 to 1939; Critchley Bros of England made and exported all kinds of knitting accessories during this period. At the same time buckles, buttons, fountain pens, cigarette holders, candlesticks and jewellery were manufactured in this material by a variety of small companies. The translucence of the material, together with rich patterning, are the characteristics of Erinoid and help in its identification even if a piece does not bear the trade name.

**Urea formaldehyde box
by Fornells**
15 x 15cm
John Jesse & Irina Laski, London
Price: £80

SYNTHETIC PLASTICS

The true synthetic plastics which most concern the collector of Art Deco plastics fall into two major categories, the formaldehydes and the polymers. It is to the first category that 'Bakelite', probably the most famous of all plastics, belongs. Formaldehyde was a by-product of the coal industry which, when combined with phenol, formed an insoluble resin. This was known about in the nineteenth century, but what was not understood at that time was how the resin could be thermoset, rendered hard and permanent. In 1907 Dr Leo Baekeland discovered the process of working phenol formaldehyde through three stages and at high temperatures and pressures; he filed his patent in 1909 (it was known as the 'heat and pressure patent') and formed the General Bakelite Co. a year later.

Two further improvements in the manufacturing technique in 1923 and 1926 – the process for ejecting Bakelite mouldings hot from the mould, and the invention of transfer moulding – added to the commercial success of the material. Thomas Edison was already using it to make gramophone records, and Westinghouse was experimenting with Bakelite as a laminate. Its superior insulating properties made it invaluable to the electrical industries in Europe and America and a natural material for the radio of the twenties and thirties. The early phenolic radio cabinets tend to be highly decorated, cast from intricate moulds with filigree speaker grills. The British Telson radio of 1928 is a perfect example of this.

By the thirties radio design was becoming more streamlined and

Philips and Ekco were using Bakelite cabinets with simplified geometric forms in keeping with the advances being made in the actual technology of the radio itself. The Ekco SH25, for example, which was a true 'wireless' set, had a stepped silhouette with formalized, faintly Egyptianesque moulding on the front. Only the speaker grille retains any trace of the earlier filigree style with its pattern of willow trees and water. The Ekco AD65 of 1934, designed by the ar-

Urea and chrome Thermos flask
Height: 25.8cm
John Jesse & Irina Laski, London
Price: £30

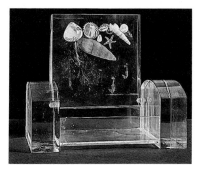

Perspex cigarette box with inlaid shells
Height: 5.8cm
John Jesse & Irina Laski, London
Price: £30

chitect Wells Coates, shows radio design at its simplest and most rational: the case is circular and the tuning scale and knobs describe two arcs which frame the round grille. The darkness of the Bakelite from which the cabinet was made emphasizes the severe stylishness of the design.

In America, plastics were first used for radio casings in 1933, when Air King Products commissioned Harold Van Doren and John Gordon Rideout to design a sharply styled but inexpensive model. The material used was Plastikon, a urea formaldehyde which could be manufactured in a variety of colours; the sombre Bakelite was not favoured by radio designers in the States.

In addition to radio cabinets Bakelite was also used by manufacturers of the new electric clocks to make housings which were tough and dramatic; Smith Sectric were making phenolic-cased clocks from the early thirties, and later models used a combination of Bakelite and urea to achieve a colour contrast and emphasize the geometric mouldings of the case.

137

In 1932 the Bakelite corporation held a symposium in the States to make industry aware of the potential of the material for consumer goods other than those made by the electrical industry. At the same time it was expanding its market in Britain by producing items which were handsome, simple to cast, with little decoration, and which relied instead on a variety of surface finishes and textures and a strong overall shape for their impact. Thus Bakelite was able to capitalize on its one drawback — that it could be produced in dark colours only. Bowls, smokers' accessories, desk sets and boxes were all made in Bakelite in the thirties. Many of them have simple, textured decoration; some rely on the high polish and dramatic colouring of the material for their appeal.

The development of cast phenolic in the late twenties gave plastics manufacturers a material which combined the toughness of bakelite with a wide range of colours and new translucency. Cast phenolic does not use a filler, and it was the wood filler in traditional Bakelite which gave it its characteristic dark colouring. Manufacturers such as the Marblette Corporation, of America, used the new material for jewellery and other decorative items. In England, Dickinson's manufactured items in cast phenolic under its trade name 'Catilin', and it is possible to find desk equipment in various colours, cocktail shakers, dressing-table sets and pieces such as stylized animal napkin rings all manufactured from Catilin.

Urea formaldehyde was first patented in 1918 but the resin was prone to bubbling and cracking in the manufacturing process. It was not

'Bandalasta' ware urea formaldehyde teapot
Height: 11cm
John Jesse & Irina Laski, London
Price: £100

Napkin rings in phenolic resin
Height (tallest): 6.6cm
John Jesse & Irina Laski, London
Price (of 3): £20

until 1921 that British Cyanides Co. formulated a method of impregnating wood flour or bleached pulp with urea formaldehyde and thiorea to produce a compound which remained stable. The resin produced by this method was transparent, which gave manufacturers enormous scope; any colour could be used and almost any effect achieved.

From 1925 a large range of items were made in urea formaldehyde, or 'Beetle', as it was more familiarly known. Some of the most elegant designs came from France where Fornells of Paris were producing boxes with lids moulded with stylish designs, the crisp precision of which looks carved rather than cast. The boxes exhibited by Fornells in the 1931 Colonial Exhibition all had exotic themes and were named, appropriately, 'Oasis', 'Cambodgiennes', and so on.

Pieces like this had a considerable influence in Britain, particularly on the boxes made by Streetly and designed by A.H. Woodfull for the Ardath cigarette company. Streetly's boxes were often made in contrasting colours with white Beetle for the lid and black 'Scarab' for the base. The same manufacturer produced a range of plastic items for Woolworth which are characterized by geometric shapes and strong colours or tonal contrasts, such as a red hexagonal sugar caster designed as a set with hexagonal green salt and pepper shakers in 1934.

Novelty items were produced in this material for the perfume indus-

> **'Cleopatra Manicure Box'**
> **reinforced phenolic resin**
> Height: 8.5cm
> John Jesse & Irina Laski, London
> Price: £30

try. The Saville Perfumery Co. commissioned Streetly to make a top hat as packaging for their 'Mischief' perfume. Two years later, in 1939, he designed and made an Easter presentation for them in the shape of an egg. Such packaging, which was seen as a 'free gift', was produced to boost the sales of luxury items on both sides of the Atlantic in the difficult economic climate of the late thirties.

Some particularly stylish cocktail and smoking accessories were also moulded from Beetle. Wilson and Gill in England made a range of cocktail shakers called 'Master Incolor', which had a smooth streamlined urea body and a chrome top that could be turned to reveal a variety of recipes through a 'window' in the rim. In the early thirties a company called Beney was making coloured cigarette lighters which it marketed under the name of Pastel-Lite and which were

139

intended to complement the phenolic and urea cigarette cases made by a number of manufacturers, including the Bakelite firm, in the thirties.

Beetle was also particularly suitable for the manufacture of colourful plastic handbags, which were produced in every possible colour and in black and white. Such bags usually consisted of two urea plates with a leather or cloth gusset. In some the plates were reinforced with a chrome frame with the fastening as part of that frame, but often the manufacturer would exploit the flexibility of plastic and mould the clip together with the body. Probably spurred on by the novelty aspect of plastic bags, the designs on them are often very amusing, incorporating popular cartoon characters or extreme versions of stylish motifs – the lightning bolt, for example, in white against a blue ground, and other forms derived from Modernist paintings.

A wide range of picnic ware and tableware was produced in Britain in Beetle under the names 'Bandalasta' (by Brookes and Adams Ltd), 'Beaconware' (by Streetly), and 'Linga Longa'. There had been attempts before to produce plastic tableware but they had proved unsuccessful because of the somewhat repellent colours of the plastics. The range of colours and colour effects which could be obtained with Beetle negated this problem and all three ranges were successful. Streetly was the first manufacturer to use paper-filled urea, which superseded thiorea in the early thirties and was given the name 'Beetleware' by that company.

Other producers of domestic equipment which utilized the new plastics included Thermos, which produced a range of pastel-coloured vacuum jugs in the thirties, and

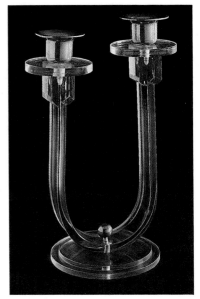

Hoover, which used a phenolic casing on its 1937 'Junior' 375, a cleaner which shows the hallmarks of American product design in its streamlined shape and clean colouring.

The American magazine *Plastic Products* re-named itself *Modern Plastics* in 1934 in response to the new attitude to manmade materials and in an attempt to overcome the lingering idea that plastics were shoddy and even at their best a poor substitute for the 'real thing'. The emphasis in the reborn journal was on the smartness of plastic and on its enormous potential as a material for product design. Plastic was an automatic choice for Walter Dorwin Teague when he designed the Kodak Brownie camera in 1935 and for Henry Dreyfuss when he produced the desk phone for Bell Telephone in 1937. From the mid-thirties, many of the large manufacturing companies used one or other of the synthetics when they redesigned their products.

If collectors are prepared to give room to pieces of industrial design they will find that some of the best examples of American Art Deco plastics are among the more stylish products of companies such as Hoover (the 150 Vacuum cleaner designed in 1936 by Dreyfuss, for example), Kodak, or the Toledo Scale Company, and many others.

The last plastic to be developed between the Wars was polymethyl methacrylate, marketed in Britain under the name 'Perspex' by ICI, and in America as 'Plexiglass' by Rohm and Haas in Philadelphia and as 'Lucite' by Du Pont. It was described by its inventor Dr Chalmers, at McGill University, Montreal, as 'plastic glass'. It was a truly transparent synthetic, capable of being manufactured in large sheets (the windows of the observation car of the train *The Coronation Scot* were made from polymethyl methacrylate in 1937)

while still being sensitive enough for the manufacture of contact lenses. In many ways it was the ideal plastic for the thirties – it expressed modernity and was 'pure' – and its potential was not overlooked by designers.

Some furniture was produced in Perspex in a style which is best described as 'machined Baroque', and these pieces were never mass produced and are extremely rare. Perspex and Plexiglass jewellery was manufactured on a large scale, as were items like light fittings, decorative boxes, trays and book ends.

In the late thirties handbags were also manufactured in transparent plastic with a design moulded on the outer surface or cut on the inside. Some examples survive which have objects – flowers, leaves and even shells – trapped in the transparent material. These were still being produced in the fifties when the designs tended to become extravagant to the point of absurdity.

'Bandalasta' ware
Height (tallest): 9.8cm
John Jesse & Irina Laski, London
Price: £100

COLLECTING PLASTICS

There is a growing interest in plastics. What was until a short time ago a very specialist field has now become much more popular, with the plastics of the twenties and thirties having a particular appeal because they are often so representative of the design of that period. To date there has not been a great deal of plastic in the larger salerooms but specialist Art Deco shops now stock the 'classic' pieces. Bandalasta, Beaconware and Linga Longa can be found in such shops, as can the boxes made by Streetly and Fornells. Plastic jewellery has become harder to find in the last three or four years but, again, the most typical pieces – bracelets, plastic and chrome necklaces and plastic pendants with beaded silk necklaces – can be found in shops and stalls dealing with general Art Deco design and in specialist jewellery shops. Items such as buckles and buttons are still reasonably easy to find simply because so many of them were made. Designs which were obviously influenced by Schiaparelli or which incorporate images of popular cartoon characters are naturally more expensive and are often collected by people who may not necessarily be interested in plastics.

Dressing-table sets in plastic are rarely complete with a tray, a pin bowl or small tray, two powder bowls and a ring-tree. If a set was produced by a mass-manufacturer like Halex it is possible to collect the pieces individually; if the set is unmarked it may have been made in small numbers and will be almost impossible to make up. Individual boxes and bowls are often very inventive in their use of materials, combinations of plastic and metal, or of different plastics, and are worth collecting for this reason. The named urea wares can be built up as sets; Bandalasta, for instance, was produced in such quantities that a patient enthusiast can be fairly sure of finding the egg-cups which match the plates and the saucers which match the cups. The larger items, teapots for example, are harder to find, as are examples of the table-lamps produced by Bandalasta in 1927.

Art Deco plastic radios present a particular problem; the great 'clas-

One of a pair of 'Carvacraft' phenolic bookends, designed by Charles Boyton
Height: 12.5cm
John Jesse & Irina Laski, London
Price: £30

sic' sets – Wells Coates' Ekco for example – are sought after by radio enthusiasts and are becoming difficult to find. But such sets do appear in the larger salerooms simply because they are recognized pieces of design rather than because they are plastic. Less important but still stylish sets can be found in America and England. In America, particularly, inexpensive sets were produced in large quantities during the thirties. Such radios are characterized by

Vogue picture record, Bakelite
Diameter: 25.3cm
Fred Marcus, M12 Antiquarius,
London
Price: £40

Urea formaldehyde box
by Fornells
15 x 15cm
John Jesse & Irina Laski, London
Price: £80

their smartness and are often sold on the basis of looks rather than function. Plastic sets are seldom to be found in working order: usually it is the valves which have been damaged and these are not easy to replace, but the early battery models from the forties, which still show clear evidence of Art Deco styling, may some-

times need only a replacement battery.

Because plastics were produced in such quantity and because only certain manufacturers are recognized and their works collected, there is still plenty of scope for the collector. Stylish and inventive pieces of all sorts turn up in junk shops and flea markets. Twenties pieces are rather easier to date than thirties items: plastics from the twenties are often elaborately moulded whereas later pieces are simpler, with a streamlined smoothness which continued in the design of commercial plastics until after the Second World War. Dickinson's, for example, were producing a cast phenolic desk set which is Art Deco in every detail but which was actually designed and made in the late 1940s; if the collector is simply looking for examples of the Art Deco style this hardly matters. 143

Bakelite

Object	Quality of manufacture	Quality of design and/or decoration	Rarity	Price (£)	Price ($)
'Smokers Friend' container for smokers' accessories, walnut finish	5	7	■ ■	5-15	10-30
cigar box, black, with moulded lid	5	7	■ ■	10-15	20-30
'Springboks' cigarette case	5	7	■ ■	5-10	10-20
set of five stacking ashtrays with holder, marked 'Stadium'	5	7	■ ■ ■	10-15	20-30
'Jaxonite' single ash tray, black with applied coloured decoration and metal cigarette rest	5	7	■ ■ ■	5-10	10-20
'Prettywell' pen and ink stand with glass fittings	5	6	■ ■	10-15	20-30
desk tidy, trefoil-shaped with hinged lid marked 'Compliments of Bakelite Ltd'	5	6	■ ■ ■	8-12	15-25
bowls and dishes	5	5	■	2-20	4-40
Thermos vacuum flask	5	7	■ ■ ■	15-30	30-50
box containing a Gillette razor	5	6	■ ■	5-10	10-20
Smith electric clock, brown with gold detailing	5	7	■ ■	5-20	10-40
radio cabinet	5	6	■ ■ ■	10-25	20-45
Murphy AD 94 (1940) radio cabinet	6	7	■ ■	30-50	50-80
Philco 444 radio cabinet	6	7	■ ■	50-85	80-140
Ekco AD 65 (Wells Coats, 1934) radio cabinet	7	8	■	100-150	160-240

Cast phenolic

Object	Quality of manufacture	Quality of design and/or decoration	Rarity	Price (£)	Price ($)
bangles, thirties	4	7	■ ■ ■	5-20	10-40
brooches, stylized animal and plant shapes	5	7	■ ■	5-20	10-40
Carvacraft pen/ink tray, C.E.Boyton	5	7	■ ■	20-40	40-60
desk blotter, en suite	5	7	■ ■	20-40	40-60
desk pad holder, en suite	5	7	■ ■	15-20	30-40
transparent acrylic and phenolic paper knife, en suite	5	7	■ ■	10-15	20-30

Qualities on a scale 1-10   ■ Rare   ■ ■ Very rare   ■ ■ ▨ Extremely rare

Object	Quality of manufacture	Quality of design and/or decoration	Rarity	Price (£)	Price ($)
Celluloid					
chrome buttons, covered with transparent celluloid, set of 6	3	5	■	2-5	3-10
large steel and gilt buttons, stylized leaf pattern, covered with transparent celluloid, set of 3	5	8	■ ■	5-15	10-30
imitation tortoiseshell manicure set, with 3 small boxes, a buffing pad and 2 implements	5	5	■ ■	10-25	20-45
imitation tortoiseshell picture frames, geometric moulding	5	6	■ ■	3-20	5-40
imitation tortoiseshell dressing-table set, tray, 3 bowls, hand mirror, hair and clothes brush	5	5	■ ■ ■	15-30 set	30-50
imitation tortoiseshell Spanish-type comb with moulded stylized flower detail	5	6	■	5-15	10-30
imitation ivory buckle, cream, heavily moulded flower pattern	5	7	■	3-10	5-20
imitation ivory bracelet, cream, heavily moulded flower pattern	4	7	■	5-15	10-30
imitation coral bracelet, heavily moulded flower pattern	4	7	■	5-15	10-30
moulded bracelet, cream, hand-tinted in flower pattern	4	8	■ ■	10-25	20-45
mirror, brush and clothes brush, green, Egyptian style, Halex	6	7	■ ■ ■	15-20 set	30-40
as above, individual pieces	5	7	■ ■	3-5	5-10
transparent and opaque xylonite powder bowls, Halex	5	7	■ ■	5-20	10-40
sheet celluloid handbag, hand-tinted with leather strap, stylized floral dec.	6	8	■ ■ ■	50-100	80-160
celluloid handbag mounts, various	5	7	■ ■	25-40	45-60
'Kelly' doll	3	5	■ ■ ■	15-40	30-60
clockwork 'Crawling Baby' doll	3	5	■ ■ ■	20-50	40-80
'Kewpie' doll	3	5	■ ■	15-40	30-60
'Bonzo' doll	3	5	■ ■	15-40	30-60

Qualities on a scale 1-10   ■ Rare   ■ ■ Very rare   ■ ■ ■ Extremely rare

Object	Quality of manufacture	Quality of design and/or decoration	Rarity	Price (£)	Price ($)
Perspex ('Lucite', 'Plexiglass')					
tea tray, clear or coloured with metal feet	4	6	▪	3-6	5-12
handbag with carved decoration	5	7	▪▪	25-50	45-80
lamp base	4	7	▪	25-100	45-160
candelabra	5	6	▪▪	25-50	45-80
Perspex and urea cigarette box	5	7	▪▪	20-40	40-60
Pressed horn					
oval box, hinged lid with incised pattern of deer and flowers	5	7	▪▪▪	20-50	40-80
card of moulded horn buttons in 3 sizes	5	4	▪▪▪	3-10	5-20
Rubber, vulcanized					
Waterman fountain pen, brown vulcanite with gold plate fittings	5	7	▪▪	25-40	45-60
Tortoiseshell					
bracelet, inlaid with gold spots	6	8	▪▪▪	50-75	80-120
Urea formaldehyde ('Beetle' and 'Scarab')					
'Bandalasta' ware bowl with hallmarked silver rim	5	8	▪	25-50	45-80
'Bandalasta' table lamp	5	7	▪	60-100	100-160
'Bandalasta' egg cups	5	7	▪▪	2-6	3-12
'Bandalasta' salt/pepper pots (pair)	5	7	▪▪	5-10	10-20
'Linga Longa' ware set of 6 tea cups and saucers, marbled orange, black and cream with matching rectangular plates	5	7	▪▪	30-50	50-80
'Linga Longa' single cup and saucer	5	7	▪▪▪	3-10	5-20
'Linga Longa' milk jug	5	7	▪▪▪	3-6	5-12

Qualities on a scale 1-10   ▪ Rare   ▪▪ Very rare   ▪▪▪ Extremely rare

Object	Quality of manufacture	Quality of design and/or decoration	Rarity	Price (£)	Price ($)
Urea formaldehyde ('Beetle' and 'Scarab') contd					
'Linga Longa' sugar basin and cover	5	7	■ ■	5-10	10-20
'Linga Longa' teapot	5	7	■	25-100	45-160
Streetly 'Beaconware' teapot	5	7	■	25-100	45-160
Streetly 'Beetleware' cup and saucer	5	7	■ ■	5-10	10-20
cigarette box, black Scarab and ivory Beetle designed by A.H. Woodfull, made by Streetly for Ardath	5	8	■	25-60	45-100
cigarette box in brown Scarab and Beetle designed by Woodfull for State Express	5	8	■	25-60	45-100
Fornells (Paris) box (L'Exposition Coloniale de Paris)	7	8	■	80-150	130-240
Fornells perfume-burner	7	8	■	80-150	130-240
Thermos vacuum jug, 1934	5	6	■ ■ ■	5-15	10-30
Wilson & Gill cocktail shaker (moulded by De La Rue)	6	8	■	25-50	45-80
Pastel-Lite cigarette lighter	4	6	■ ■	5-10	10-20
clock	5	6	■	5-50	10-80

Qualities on a scale 1-10   ■ Rare   ■ ■ Very rare   ■ ■ ■ Extremely rare

CHAPTER EIGHT

DECORATIVE SCULPTURE

Hagenauer wood and
metal bust. Sold: Christie's
South Kensington, London,
19/9/86. Price: £968.

temporary avant-garde sculpture have not been recorded, but Brancusi considered sculptured nude bodies (which abound in his compatriot's *œuvre*) to be 'less sightly than toads'. Yet both artists created icons of the twenties – Chiparus's models of flappers and dancing girls, and Brancusi's *Sophisticated Young Lady*, a portrait of Nancy Cunard done in 1925.

BRONZE AND IVORY FIGURES

The work of the avant-garde sculptors such as Brancusi, Arp, Lipchitz, Miklos and Laurens is, of course, unaffordable, and so are most bronze and ivory figures. 'Chryselephantine' figures (a term derived from the Greek words for gold and ivory), which combine carved ivory and bronze – often chased and gilded, silvered or patinated and frequently cold-painted – are nearly always very expensive, even if unsigned. In fact, generally speaking, there have been so many fakes produced over the last ten years or so, that it would be unwise to expect or accept a bronze and ivory figure at a 'bargain' price. Even figures such as saccharine toddlers (which it is hard to imagine anybody coveting), which have precisely nothing to do with Art Deco, command considerable sums. There is, however, a wealth of decorative sculpture which is essentially Art Deco, often of good quality, and considerably less expensive. There are many figures made in bronze only, or spelter, without any ivory parts, which are much cheaper. By the same token, figures that are made of ivory only are also less expensive. The combination of the two materials gives chryselephantine sculpture a flashy quality which costs dear.

Alabaster bust on marble base
Height: 40cm
Mikael Hallström/Michael Brazil,
P12-14 Antiquarius, London
Price: £350

Between the two World Wars sculpture was produced in an enormous number of different styles. At one end of the range stood the works of Constantin Brancusi, whose *The Beginning of the World* (1924) is a pure, egg-shaped form; at the other end were the creations of Demetre Chiparus, a master of bronze and ivory figure sculpture. The two artists had little in common beyond the coincidence that they were both Romanians living and working in Paris. Chiparus's feelings about con-

FIGURES OF FASHION

There is a large group of figures, including nearly all the bronze and ivory ones, which are too naturalistic in style to be correctly called Art Deco. They can be classified as such only to the extent that their subject matter is drawn from the people and pastimes of the twenties and thirties.

Bronze figure
Height: 33.5cm
Jonathan Hunter Smith, N2/3
Antiquarius, London
Price: £200

Like a three-dimensional version of *Vogue* or *Harper's*, they provide an account of modes and mores among the rich during the inter-War years: women are represented with their hair bobbed, shingled, or cropped *à la garçonne*; they are dressed in fashionable garments such as Chanel jersey suits, tea-gowns, culottes or pyjamas. Very often the clothes are painted with typical Art Deco patterns. The sculptured ladies are seen leaving the opera in long, fur-collared coats and cloche hats, or perched on bar-stools attending to their make-up, or smoking a cigarette in a holder. There are many figures of ladies with dogs, particularly borzois. It seems to have been the Marchesa Luisa Casati who first made it chic to be seen with two or three borzois, their sleek, attenuated limbs complementing her own lissom figure. 'Dogs are now so fashionable,' wrote a commentator in *Vogue* during the twenties, 'that one wonders why they are not sold by the couturiers.'

DANCING FIGURES

There is also an endless sucession of figures of dancing girls. Often they are balanced on one foot, which seems to have been a matter of some self-congratulation among those who produced the figures. They carry scarves, fans, hoops, balls, cymbals or tambourines – even a parakeet or two. They usually wear a very abbreviated version of ethnic costume: Nubian, Assyrian, Hindu, Mexican, Argentinian etc. They too, however, represent twenties high life, having been modelled on the girls who performed in the popular revues of the time: Ziegfeld's *Follies* in New York; C.B. Cochran's shows in London; the

151

Perhaps some of the more exotic costumes worn by these figurines were inspired by the elaborate outfits created for the countless fancy-dress balls held at the time. Groups of two or three nude or scantily clad females dancing in symmetrical formation may well have been derived from the illustrations for a 1923 *Vogue* article written by Margaret Morris, whose theories of dance were based on the natural movements and positions depicted in Classical Greek art.

SPORTING FIGURES

The twenties obsession with sport is well represented in the gallery of these sculptured figures. The *haut monde* had taken to spending the winter months at ski resorts, and there are several figures of skiers and skaters. The French sculptor Marcel Bouraine produced a sculpture of two skaters entitled *At Chamonix*, and Bruno Zach of Berlin made a model of a five-man bobsleigh travelling at speed. There are many tennis players and several golfers including a lady playing the game in a swimsuit and another driving off while standing on one leg. There are ladies running, fencing and throwing javelins (an unofficial feminine Olympics was held at Monte Carlo in 1923). Only rugby football seems to have been treated by the sculptors as a male preserve.

**Silvered bronze figure
by Pierre Laurel**
Height: 44cm
Sold: Phillips, London, 13/3/86
Price: £935

Folies Bergère in Paris; and the Haller Revue in Berlin. Figures have been identified which represent specific performers. The American dancer Georgia Graves, for example, who performed her bubble-dance at the *Folies Bergère* in 1930 was sculptured by Godard, and Ada May, a star of one of Cochran's revues, modelled for Ferdinand Preiss.

Following the excavation in 1922 of the tomb of Tutankhamun at Luxor, decorative motifs from ancient Egyptian art were widely used by Art Deco designers. The sculptors were not slow to exploit the craze, but their fundamental attachment to academic art was not unduly affected. One of the assets of Egyptian ornament, as far as they were concerned, was the characteristic head-band in the form of a cobra. This allowed their otherwise nude females to be readily identified as hand maidens of King Tut.

Several figures were mounted on pyramidal bases, a further acknow-ledgement of the current fad. The plinth is often the only part of these sculptures which is an intrinsically Art Deco design. Plinth shapes included cubes, cylinders, spheres, ziggurats and wedges, as well as pyramids, and were usually made of onyx or marble or a combination of the two. Green onyx was particularly favoured, often in combination with black marble; together they make a rich contrast to the dark brown and the off-white of the bronze and ivory statuette above. Many other shades of marble were used, often arranged in geometrical patterns typical of Art Deco, such as the sunburst motif. However, the abstract pattern on the plinth sometimes clashes stylistically with the minute realistic detail of the sculptured figure above it. A nadir of aesthetic absurdity was reached in a naturalistic, carved ivory female nude by Preiss sitting demurely

among circular and rectangular marble shapes which make up a clock-case inspired by Bauhaus constructivism rather than the academic tradition.

BERLIN SCULPTURE

In 1906 the ivory carver Ferdinand Preiss opened a workshop in Berlin, where he was joined, four years later, by Robert Kionsek of the Gladenbeck bronze foundry. At the outbreak of war in 1914 the firm, known as PK, employed about half a dozen craftsmen. During the twenties and thirties, Preiss designed a great number of figures which were manufactured in bronze and ivory, and a few – much cheaper then and now – which were carved in ivory alone. The latter, generally female nudes, sometimes have a compactness of contour

Silvered bronze figure by Maurice Guiraud-Rivière
Height: 37cm
Sold: Sotheby's, London, 16/5/86
Price: £528

together with a delicacy of carving which almost attains to the artistic quality of Japanese *netsuke*.

In 1929 PK took over the firm of Rosenthal & Maeder which manufactured bronze and ivory figures modelled by Philippe (a sculptor from Vienna), Otto Poerzl and Dorothea Charol, among others. Charol and another sculptor, Bruno Zach, made several figures evoking the smuttier side of Berlin life during the Weimar Republic and the Third Reich, apparently inspired by Krafft-Ebing as much as by the Kamasutra.

VIENNESE SCULPTURE

In Vienna, the firm of Friederich Goldscheider manufactured bronze and ivory figures during the 1920s and the 1930s, most of them modelled by the sculptor Joseph Lorenzl. Some were produced in bronze and ivory, some in ivory alone, and many in gilt or silvered bronze, or in spelter. Although his subjects were the usual dancing girls and fashionably dressed ladies, Lorenzl's figures are more stylized than their German counterparts – the tubular aspect of the twenties female figure is exaggerated and the limbs are elongated. The formal composition of Lorenzl's statuettes is often a subtle arrangement of serpentine curves; they exude Viennese sophistication and charm.

A much greater degree of stylization is found in the sculpture produced by the Argentor and Hagenauer workshops in Vienna. Some of their themes, such as female nudes and gymnasts, are drawn from the repertoire of the bronze and ivory sculptors, but the treatment is always quite different. Humans and animals are reduced to simplified

forms; some are rounded and fluid, some angular and spiky (like so much Austrian Art Deco) and some practically Cubist. The figures range from

Spelter figural lamp
Height: 42.6cm
Hilary Conquy, N6 Antiquarius,
London
Price: £265

animals less than an inch high, usually made out of chromed metal, to two-feet-high figures and busts in metal or carved wood, often with stands of copper or brass.

PARISIAN SCULPTURE

In Paris three principal firms were involved in the commissioning and distribution of decorative sculpture. One of them, Etling, handled the statues of Demetre Chiparus and Claire-Jeanne-Roberte Colinet. Bronze and ivory figures by these two artists are always very expensive, but less expensive works by both were reproduced in patinated, silvered or gilt bronze, or in zinc-based alloys, and there are Chiparus figures carved entirely out of ivory. The style of Chiparus's work is usually quite naturalistic, although sometimes the arrangement of folds in the costumes has been slightly stylized. Perhaps the most distinctive feature of his figures is the often elaborate treatment of the costumes, as well as their spectacular design. Colinet's career started in Belgium at the turn of the century, and her style never really developed beyond an Art Nouveau idiom.

Other artists who sometimes worked for Etling were A. Becquerel, Marcel Bouraine, Lucille Sevin, Geneviève Granger and Maurice Guiraud-Rivière. But their style is distinct from the naturalism of most decorative sculpture – their figures are more formal, more static. Drapery tends to be classical rather than modish; its folds are rendered in parallel and zigzag lines in low relief. Hair has sometimes been modelled on the fashionable styling of the day but has often been reduced to parallel, wavy lines which stream back

Bronze figure on onyx tray
Height: 24cm
Jonathan Hunter Smith, N2/3
Antiquarius, London
Price: £275

from the forehead. This degree of formalization and abstraction contrasts with the naturalism of most bronze and ivory sculpture and is much more consistent with the true Art Deco style.

The Goldscheider firm in Paris, quite independent of the Viennese concern, produced and distributed decorative sculpture in this more Art Deco manner. Some of the sculptors who worked for the firm were Pierre Traverse, Raoul Lamourdedieu, Sybille May, Alexander Kelety and Pierre le Faguays. The last named also made figures which were distributed through Max le Verrier's shop in the rue du Théâtre. Le Verrier was a sculptor himself who sold statuettes, figural lamps and bookends by, among others, Raymond Guerbe,

155

Fayral, Marcel Bouraine and Pierre le Faguays, as well as his own work. These sculptures, cast in various alloys, sometimes combined with carved ivory, are very Art Deco in manner. Classical nudes, formalized draperies and garlands of stylized flowers are typical features.

This sort of Art Deco sculpture was very much in evidence at the Paris Exhibition of 1925. The pavilion of the cabinet-maker Ruhlmann, for instance, featured statues and reliefs in this style by Joseph Bernard and Charles Despiau. Their heavy-limbed nudes suggest that behind their sculpture lies the influence of Aristide Maillol, whose *Bather with Drap-*

ery had been shown at the 1921 Salon. 'Maillol's statue', a critic had declared then, 'is arousing the enthusiasm of every visitor'. Some sculptors whose works reflect Maillol's genius were Henry Arnold, Joé Descomps, Raphael Schwartz and Henri Fugère.

The sculpture of Emile-Antoine Bourdelle, whose work was also fea-

---

Silvered bronze bookends by Maurice Guiraud-Rivière
Height: 17.25cm
Sold: Sotheby's, London, 16/5/86
Price: £528

tured in the Ruhlmann pavilion, had been another formative influence on the Art Deco style of decorative sculpture. His bronze *Heracles the Archer*, exhibited at the Salon of 1910, was the sire of statuettes by Kelety (*The Release*) and le Faguays (*Signal Man*), as well as a myriad of *Dianas* and other female archers. Bourdelle, too, seems to have been the first (in modern times) to represent the hair streaming out behind the head in wavy parallel lines. He had shown the hair of *The Muses* like this in his 1912 reliefs for the façade of the Théâtre des Champs-Elysées. These figures in turn had been inspired by the dancing of Isadora

Hagenauer metal masks
Height (tallest): 21.5cm
Sold: Sotheby's, New York, 20/6/86
Price: $1100

Hagenauer silvered bronze horse
Height: 5cm
Mikael Hallström/Michael Brazil,
P12-14 Antiquarius, London
Price: £110

Bronze medal Chicago World's Fair 1933
Diameter: 3.8cm
Fred Marcus, M12 Antiquarius,
London
Price: £25

Duncan. In another relief from the same series, Bourdelle had modelled the figures symbolizing dancing on Isadora Duncan and Nijinsky.

Like Bourdelle, François Pompon had worked in Rodin's studio for a number of years. At the 1922 Salon d'Automne in Paris he exhibited a marble statue of a polar bear which was widely acclaimed and opened a new chapter in the history of animal sculpture. The considerable degree of stylization, as well as the surface smoothness of Pompon's figures, marked a decisive break from the traditional manner of the nineteenth-century *animaliers*, and soon there emerged a host of followers.

Armand Petersen, Maurice Prost, Georges-Lucien Guyot, Gaston le Bourgeois and Edouard-Marcel Sandoz are among those who made stylized animal figures, although they did not generally depart as far from

naturalism as Pompon often did. Panthers were a favoured subject, probably for their distinctive shape and smooth hair – perhaps also because the animal's sleek form and predatory air suggest the vamp, just as the svelte figure and nervous tension of the greyhound and borzoi symbolized the flapper. Bronzes by these sculptors are comparatively rare but not necessarily too expensive. Many sculptures of stylized animals and birds were made as car mascots by, for instance, A. Becquerel, Marcel Bouraine and Maurice Guiraud-Rivière; they are usually made of chromed metal, brass or other alloys.

AMERICAN SCULPTURE

In the USA the equivalent to Parisian firms like Goldscheider, Etling and le Verrier was the Gorham company which operated a bronze foundry at Providence, Rhode Island, and a retail outlet on Fifth Avenue in New York City. None of the figures that Gorham produced incorporated ivory, but they were close to contemporary French decorative sculpture in subject matter and style; most of the sculptors working for Gorham were Americans who had studied in Paris. A typical Gorham bronze was a table-fountain by Maude Sherwood Jewett with two classical nude

Bronze cockerel
Height: 17.8cm
V24, Antiquarius, London
Price: £44

Bronze panther
Length: 67cm
Sold: Phillips, London, 13/3/86
Price: £990

figures of a youth and a maiden leaning backwards from the waist and clasping each other's wrists. Other artists from whom Gorham commissioned sculpture were Allan Clark, Mabel Conkling, Laura Gardin Fraser, Jeanette Ramson, Alexander Phimister Proctor (the 'sculptor in buckskin' who specialized in Wild West subjects) and Harriet W. Frismuth. Ms Frismuth had studied under Rodin and the nude figurines which she sculpted were one of Gorham's best-selling lines; she also modelled *Speed*, a car mascot in the form of a nude female figure with stylized wings and hair streaming behind her head in conventional wavy lines.

One of the influences on many American sculptors during the 1920s was the work of Paul Manship, but his bronzes of mythological subjects are rare and very expensive. The same applies to the stylized animals, particularly panthers, modelled by Bruce Moore. The avant-garde sculpture of John Storrs is also beyond the means of the modest collector.

BRITISH SCULPTURE

In Britain during the twenties and thirties little bronze casting seems to have been done. Direct carving in wood and stone were in favour with most of the sculptors and critics. Dora Gordine, whose Oriental heads such as *Chinese Philosopher* have an Art Deco flavour, had her bronzes cast in Paris. Another sculptor, Antony Gibbons Grinling, made bronzes of nude dancers which were sometimes mounted on stepped marble bases. He also designed a room of tubular steel sculpture and furniture for Whiteley's, the London department store. Eric Gill, Gilbert Bayes and Richard Garbe probably produced the most stylish Art Deco sculpture made in Britain, but examples of their work, mostly carved in wood or stone and consequently rare, are very expensive.

MEDALS AND PLAQUES

Medals and small plaques make an interesting and comparatively cheap area of collecting. Work by some of the great Art Deco sculptors can be acquired in this way without having to raise a bank loan. For instance, Richard Garbe made several small bronze plaques, and Gilbert Bayes was a notable medallist. One of Bayes's medals was issued in celebration of the Cunard liner *Queen Mary's* maiden voyage in 1937. In France medals were made for the maiden voyages of the liners *Paris, Ile-de-France* and *Normandie*. The most renowned French medallist was Pierre Turin who sculpted medals for the 1925 Exhibition in Paris. Jean Vernon made bronze plaques which often featured female figures, doves and garlands of flowers in a style reminiscent of paintings by Jean Dupas. Marcel Renard and Maurice Delannoy were two other French sculptors who made several medals and plaques. The twin brothers Jan and Jöel Martel from Nantes made more or less Cubist sculpture which is rare and expensive, but they also produced a number of small plaques which are generally much cheaper and often very stylish.

In 1930 the Society of Medalists was founded in the USA with the object of promoting the art of the medal. Among the medals which the Society commissioned over the following decade were Paul Manship's *Hail to Dionysus* (1930), Anthony de Francisci's *Creation* (1935) and Albert Stewart's *Peace* (1936), to mention only the most stylish ones. Several medals were issued by the larger industrial firms to celebrate various milestones in their histories; these are often in a Modernist style. For example, NBC issued a medal for is tenth anniversary in 1936, and another was made to commemorate the twenty-fifth anniversary of General Motors in 1933; this was designed by Norman Bel Geddes, who created some of the earliest streamlined automobiles.

**Painted metal figural lamp
by Raymond Guerbe**
Height: 50cm
Sold: Phillips, London, 19/6/86
Price: £825

Object	Quality of manufacture	Quality of design and/or decoration	Rarity	Price (£)	Price ($)
Anon.					
metal figure	5	5	■	50-150	80-240
painted metal figure	5	5	■	75-200	120-320
bronze figure plain/gilt/silvered	5	5	■	250-500	400-800
ivory figure	5	5	■	100-300	160-480
bronze and ivory figure	5	5	■	200-500	320-800
bronze medal	5	5	■	20-60	400-100
Argentor					
animal group, chrome/wood	8	8	■ ■ ■	500-750	800-1200
Arnold, Henry					
small bronze figure, female nude	8	7	■ ■ ■	250-500	400-800
large bronze figure, female nude	8	7	■ ■ ■	600-900	1000-1440
Bayes, Gilbert					
bronze medal	8	8	■ ■	40-100	60-160
Bofill, Antoine					
bronze and ivory figure of a child	7	2	■ ■	300-500	480-800
Bory, J.					
bronze figure of a vulture	8	6	■ ■ ■	250-350	400-560
Chiparus, Demetre					
painted metal figure	7	6	■ ■	600-900	1000-1440
gilt bronze figure	7	6	■ ■	750-1000+	1200-1600+
Colinet, Claire-Jeanne-Roberte					
painted bronze figure	7	5	■ ■	750-1000+	1200-1600+
Delannoy, Maurice					
medal	9	7	■ ■	30-100	50-160

Qualities on a scale 1-10   ■ Rare   ■ ■ Very rare   ■ ■ ■ Extremely rare

Object	Quality of manufacture	Quality of design and/or decoration	Rarity	Price (£)	Price ($)
Descomps, Joé					
ivory figure	7	6	■ ■	750-1000+	1200-1600+
painted bronze figure	7	6	■ ■	750-1000+	1200-1600+
Fugère, Henri					
silvered bronze figure	7	7	■ ■	250-500	400-800
Garbe, Richard					
bronze plaquette	9	8	■ ■ ■	150-400	240-640
Geddes, Norman Bel					
medal	9	9	■ ■ ■	200-400	320-640
Godard, A.					
bronze figure	7	6	■ ■ ■	750-1000	1200-1600
Gorham					
bronze figure	8	6	■ ■	500-1000+	800-1600+
Guerbe, Raymond					
painted metal figural lamp	6	8	■ ■ ■	600-900	1000-1440
Guiraud-Rivière, Maurice					
silvered bronze figure	7	7	■ ■	500-750	800-1200
silvered bronze figural bookends (pair)	7	7	■ ■	450-700	720-1120
silvered bronze figural lamp	7	7	■ ■	500-1000	800-1600
Hagenauer					
small metal figure	6	8	■ ■	50-100	80-160
wood and metal bust	7	8	■ ■	800-1000+	1280-1600+
metal mask	7	8	■ ■ ■	300-600	480-1000
wood figure	7	8	■ ■	250-500	400-800
medium-sized metal figure	7	8	■ ■	400-800	640-1280
large metal figure	7	8	■ ■	700-1000+	1120-1600+

Qualities on a scale 1-10   ■ Rare   ■ ■ Very rare   ■ ■ ■ Extremely rare

Object	Quality of manufacture	Quality of design and/or decoration	Rarity	Price (£)	Price ($)
Hussmann, A.					
gilt bronze and ivory figure	7	5	■ ■ ■	600-900	1000-1440
Jaeger, E.					
gilt bronze and ivory figure	7	5	■ ■	350-700	560-1120
bronze figure	7	6	■ ■	500-750	800-1200
Laurel, Pierre					
silvered bronze figure	7	6	■ ■	750-1000	1200-1600
Le Faguays, Pierre					
bronze figure	8	7	■ ■	600-900	1000-1440
Lorenzl, Josef					
bronze/gilt bronze figure	7	7	■	500-1000+	800-1600+
bronze and ivory figure	7	7	■	500-1000+	800-1600+
painted bronze figure	7	7	■	500-800	800-1280
Manship, Paul					
medal	9	7	■ ■ ■	100-200	160-320
Meier, E.					
bronze and ivory group	7	5	■ ■ ■	800-1000	1280-1600
Philippe, P.					
painted bronze figure	7	5	■ ■	400-800	640-1280
Preiss, Ferdinand					
bronze and ivory figure	7	6	■	900-1000+	1440-1600+
ivory figure	7	6	■ ■	900-1000+	1440-1600+
Prost, Maurice					
bronze figure	8	8	■ ■ ■	750-1000+	1200-1600+

Qualities on a scale 1-10   ■ Rare   ■ ■ Very rare   ■ ■ ■ Extremely rare

Object	Quality of manufacture	Quality of design and/or decoration	Rarity	Price (£)	Price ($)
Sosson, L ivory figure	7	5	■ ■	400-700	640-1120
Turin, Pierre medal	8	8	■ ■	75-150	120-240
Weisler, F. bronze figure	7	5	■ ■ ■	350-600	560-1000
Zach, Bruno bronze figure	7	6	■ ■	900-1000+	1440-1600+

Qualities on a scale 1-10   ■ Rare   ■ ■ Very rare   ■ ■ ■ Extremely rare

Index

Pages in italics contain illustrations